PLANNING FOR YOUR RETIREMENT

Tony Lamb is one of the country's most skilled fighters for senior citizens' rights and an outspoken retirement expert. In his extraordinary career as a scientist he invented the world's first practical solar cell, the first light meter, the automatic camera, and the electric eye; he holds over two hundred patents. Now in his mid-seventies, Lamb is a nationwide spokesman for the aged and a regular contributor to *Modern Maturity* magazine. He lives in Newbury Park, California.

Dave Duffy is a free-lance writer who lives in Oxnard, California.

PLANNING
FOR YOUR
RETIREMENT

TONY LAMB
AND DAVE DUFFY

PENGUIN BOOKS

Penguin Books Ltd, Harmondsworth,
Middlesex, England
Penguin Books, 625 Madison Avenue,
New York, New York 10022, U.S.A.
Penguin Books Australia Ltd, Ringwood,
Victoria, Australia
Penguin Books Canada Limited, 2801 John Street,
Markham, Ontario, Canada L3R 1B4
Penguin Books (N.Z.) Ltd, 182–190 Wairau Road,
Auckland 10, New Zealand

First published in the United States of America
under the title *The Retirement Threat*
by J. P. Tarcher, Inc., 1977
First published in Canada
under the title *The Retirement Threat*
by Macmillan of Canada 1977
Published in Penguin Books
under the title *Planning for Your Retirement* 1978

LIBRARY OF CONGRESS CATALOGING IN PUBLICATION DATA
Lamb, Tony.
Planning for your retirement.
First published (c1977) under title:
The retirement threat.
Bibliography: p. 163.
Includes index.
1. Retirement—United States.   I. Duffy, Dave, joint author.   II. Title.
[HQ1062.L29 1978a]   301.43'5   78–5069
ISBN 0 14 046.356 9

Printed in the United States of America by
Offset Paperback Mfrs., Inc., Dallas, Pennsylvania
Set in Times Roman

*For Fred Johnston
and the friends he left behind*

CONTENTS

THE STRAIGHT TALK OF TONY LAMB
By Dave Duffy   x

1 A GLIMPSE INTO THE FUTURE:
  What Your Retirement May Hold   1

2 THE GREAT RETIREMENT LIE   10

3 YOUR RETIREMENT BUDGET: How Much
  Will You Need to Live On?   23

4 SOCIAL SECURITY, PENSIONS, AND SAVINGS:
  Less Certain Than You Think   33

5 PLAN TO HAVE MONEY: Winning Your War
  Against Inflation   45

6 PLAN TO WORK: Preparing for Your
  Second Career   77

7 PLAN TO BE HEALTHY: Staying Active
  in Body and Mind   94

8 PLAN TO FIGHT: A Short Course
  in Senior Advocacy   114

9 A MODEL OF WHAT CAN BE ACCOMPLISHED:
   Ventura County, California   134

10 A GLIMPSE INTO A BETTER FUTURE   155

RECOMMENDED READING   163

APPENDIX A   Government Volunteer and
             Employment Programs for
             Retired People   164

APPENDIX B   Other Employment for
             Retired People   165

APPENDIX C   Health Associations   166

APPENDIX D   General Organizations
             Pertaining to Senior Citizens   167

APPENDIX E   National, Regional, and State
             Offices on Aging   169

INDEX   174

ACKNOWLEDGMENTS

This book owes the greatest debt to the following people:

Irene Lamb Brown, for permission to excerpt material from her senior survival and senior advocacy manuals, which she wrote for retired people in Ventura County, Calif.;

Julie Robertson, for research and editorial assistance;

John Silveira, for helping research financial matters for Chapter 5;

Brian Williams, for overall editorial guidance and encouragement;

Victoria Pasternack, for organization;

Lucy Barajikian, for copy editing;

Jeremy Tarcher, the publisher, for envisioning the book.

Thanks also are due Gene Vier, Kati Acosta, Leo Aaltonen, Rita Garfield, Sue Butler, Olga Robertson, Fred Brennion, Brenda Trombley, Maggie McKean, Joy Blankinship, and Abraham Hurwitz.

THE STRAIGHT TALK OF TONY LAMB
By Dave Duffy

If you're in your forties, it's not too late.

If you're in your fifties, you'd better hustle to make up for lost time and start planning your retirement years.

If you're in your sixties or over, you've probably got problems—even if you don't know it—and this book may be your last best hope.

This is a book for men and women who have been sold the Great Retirement Lie—that retirement is something you don't have to worry about until you are in your sixties, and then your pension or Uncle Sam will take care of you.

That is simply not so. Despite Social Security, Medicare, and private pension plans, retirement is no more secure today than it was in the 1930s—maybe even less. As you will see, it isn't even secure for middle-class and upper-middle-class people, who tend to think of themselves as prepared for those years. Because they have been used to a higher standard of living, the fact is that those are just the people who find the changes even more disastrous than other working people. Your retirement years will be what you yourself make them. That is the straight talk from Tony Lamb.

I met Tony Lamb in 1973 while I was working as a reporter for the *Oxnard Press Courier* in Ventura County,

California. He is an extraordinary man, a world-famous inventor who has since turned his considerable talents toward helping prevent the impoverishment of the elderly. As a junior engineer at the age of twenty-eight he invented the world's first practical solar cell, the small, light-sensitive disc now used on satellites to convert sunlight to electricity. He also invented the first light meter, the automatic camera, the electric eye, and instruments that enabled planes to fly at night for the first time. During World War II he invented the first target-guided bomb. All in all, he accumulated more than 200 patents and made millions of dollars of profit for the companies for whom he worked.

Since his retirement in 1971, Tony has taken up a new career coordinating services for senior citizens in Ventura County, a sprawling coastal area of nine cities which lies between Los Angeles and Santa Barbara. Applying the same remarkable abilities that made him successful in industry, he has been able to show older people how to extract the maximum benefits owed them by society, how to penetrate obtuse bureaucracies, and, most importantly, how to organize themselves for political power in their community. He has been appointed by California Governor Jerry Brown to a statewide council on legal services for poor people and has become a nationwide spokesman for the aged, appearing in many print, radio, and television interviews. He has worked with and counseled more than 50,000 retired persons.

Planning for Your Retirement, which Tony asked me to write with him, contains the essential ingredients of his success as a straighttalker, a problem solver for the retired. In many ways *Planning for Your Retirement* is two books. The first is an effort to convince people in their middle years of the need to examine what their retirement life might be and to understand that they must plan now to make it what they want it to be.

The second book is addressed to those same people in their middle years as well as to those near retirement or already retired. It is a call to action for those two groups— whose ages span as much as forty years—to organize and fight for all the services that they will require to live out their lives in dignity.

In each of his lectures, interviews, and workshops on retirement planning, Tony raises vital questions that you must answer now. If you're not yet retired, consider whether you will be able to maintain your standard of living in retirement and, if so, how do you prepare yourself to compete in the severely limited job market for retired people? How should you plan for your spouse in the event of your death? How should you prepare yourself to be happy in the world of the retired?

This book is also a primer for the retired of today who never had the benefit of sound retirement advice. Not only does it explain how to deal with such things as Social Security and Medicare, it is also a guide to help you regain the political and economic power that you lost upon retirement.

No matter who you are—office worker, mechanic, teacher, union member, salesman, or even if you are already retired—this book has the facts that could prevent you from taking the greatest downward slide of your life.

PLANNING
FOR YOUR
RETIREMENT

1 A GLIMPSE INTO THE FUTURE: What Your Retirement May Hold

Your retirement can be a dream or a nightmare. It depends on how you plan.

My name is Tony Lamb, and I'm seventy-three years old. I'd like to tell you a little about myself, since my experience could help you avoid the catastrophe of retirement by showing you how to plan for it—now.

For most of my adult life I worked as a scientist and inventor for Weston Electric Company of New Jersey. During my thirty years with the company, I rose through the ranks to become one of the firm's vice-presidents and, as a result, I enjoyed all the financial rewards and status that such a position commands.

My wife, Irene, and I lived comfortably in Hillside, New Jersey. By the time I reached fifty-five we had paid off the mortgage on our large house and had the financial freedom to enjoy various luxuries and expensive vacations. Our two children had already completed their educations, had married, become wonderful adults, and were planning their own families. Irene and I were both healthy and had every reason to be deeply satisfied with our lives. We were as secure in our happiness as any couple could expect to be.

But I have always been a cautious man, so in 1958, at age fifty-five, I decided to take stock of my career. I was ten years away from retirement and wanted to be sure my house was in order, so I carefully examined my present and projected financial standing.

What I found shocked me. As financially rewarding as my thirty years at Weston had been, I discovered that once I retired, the income that supported my comfortable world would not only cease abruptly, but that I had neither an adequate pension nor any retirement medical policy. I then investigated the Social Security benefits I would be entitled to when I retired, and made a discovery I've had confirmed a thousand times over. Social Security isn't security; it's poverty. The facts were that Social Security, plus my pension, would amount to a fraction of the income I had become accustomed to living on. Like most successful business people, I had grown used to an ever-increasing standard of living and had never imagined that I might ever need to give it up.

What disturbed me even more was the discovery that Irene, my companion since I was twenty-five years old, would be in even worse shape when I retired if I were to die before her. Not only would my company pension stop upon my death but her Social Security would be reduced as well. That prospect really frightened me. Memories of my own youth sprang to mind when, during the severe New Jersey winter of 1916, my family plunged into poverty.

It began when my father, who had owned a successful contracting business, died suddenly of pneumonia. Within a year, my father's business went bankrupt, my mother was forced to sell our home, and the family moved into a poor section of Newark. At the age of fifteen, I had to drop out of school and go to work as a messenger boy while my mother took in sewing from neighbors. The memory of my mother going hungry so her three young children could eat will never be erased from my mind. I had tasted poverty before and didn't want another bite.

Now all these years later, that problem of whether there would be enough to live on was again an issue. For the first time I seriously faced the question of what would happen if I were to fall ill or die within a few years after I retired. Would my wife experience the same poverty that befell my mother? The likelihood of it happening haunted me. I knew that women outlived men an average of eight years, and I was already five years older than my wife. In terms of life expectancy, then, there was more than a decade of difference between us.

I discussed retirement with friends I had worked with for years and found that few knew much about their company pension plan or about Social Security, nor did they seem very concerned about learning. Retirement was just too far away for most of them to worry about it.

As for me, although I was healthy and felt I could go on working forever, I was worried. So I decided to do something immediately to secure the future for my wife. Time was on my side. I was only fifty-five.

The first step I took was to resign from Weston, since the retirement benefits were simply inadequate. The move shocked my friends and colleagues, but Irene was behind me. I also knew from my previous contacts in the industry that I could improve my position. I was interviewed by five major engineering companies, then accepted a job at the Curtiss-Wright Corporation. Although some of the other companies had offered higher salaries, Curtiss-Wright had the best pension plan, which would provide for my wife if I died, and provided the best medical policies, stock options, and other fringe benefits, which I could take with me into retirement. Because I was an executive in the prime of my abilities with ten years still left before retirement, the company agreed I could qualify for all retirement benefits within five years.

At the age of sixty-two, after qualifying for full Curtiss-Wright pension benefits, I retired again to make more money by hiring out as a private consultant and by marketing my own ideas. As a consultant, I earned $300 a day plus expenses. As a private inventor, I developed several tiny industrial and medical thermometers that were very profitable. Before I retired again at age sixty-eight, I had worked myself into a strong financial position.

In the end things did not turn out as I had anticipated. The prime motive for all of my planning had been to secure Irene's future, but in 1965 she died of cancer at the age of fifty-seven. The beneficiary of all my careful planning turned out to be me.

Today I'm retired, healthy, and financially secure. But my security comes not from profits from my scientific achievements nor from my forty-three years of continual employment. It is from my own personal planning.

Now let me tell you about some people—some even formerly wealthy—who did not plan fully for their retirement years.

RETIREMENT MADE THEM POOR

In 1971 I moved to Southern California, regarded by many as the ideal retirement spot. I bought a home in the hills of Conejo Valley, near Thousand Oaks, a beautiful residential area overlooking the Santa Monica Mountains that stretch out to the Pacific Ocean. It seemed like paradise. I felt very lucky.

But in this area I met people for whom retirement wasn't like paradise. It was hell. I found out about it one day while exploring the valley where I came upon an area that real estate salesmen had never bothered to show me, one of the oldest sections in the valley, occupied mainly by old retired people living in battered houses. Wearing dirty, worn-out clothing, they sat with unsmiling faces on broken-down front stoops. Some, I found out later, had no telephone, no radio, not even a refrigerator to keep their food cold. Their poverty was staggering.

I struck up some conversations and was invited inside to talk. In one old widow's house the plywood ceiling in her kitchen sagged so low she had to stoop to walk under it. It had been that way for more than a year, she said, but she didn't have the money to get it fixed. Her toilet had been plugged up for six months, and there was no electricity in the bathroom. Her husband, a construction worker, had died fifteen years earlier. She was now struggling to survive on a Social Security check of $105 a month. I found out later that she could have gotten $296 a month from Social Security to live on, but she didn't know how to apply for the money.

An old widower invited me in for a beer. He took the beer out of a refrigerator that didn't work. When he opened the beer, it shot up to the ceiling from the heat. He said the refrigerator hadn't worked in years and he'd gotten used to warm beer. He told me he had been a foreman in a factory in the Midwest, but had retired eleven years before and was now living on Social Security and a $60-a-month pension.

Although most of the people I talked to had never been wealthy, poverty was a new experience for them—and certainly not what they had anticipated retirement to be. They had all worked hard and enjoyed middle-class living—or better—before they retired. They had expected that to continue. But they were a long way from comfort now. Some of them a long, long way.

For example, one man, now in his seventies, had been a crackerjack retail salesman. He told me he was a "high roller" during his prime and lived in the plushest apartments money could buy. One year he earned sales commissions of nearly $50,000. But he had spent every cent he made. He had never invested in any income-producing annuities, stocks, or property of any kind, and he had never worked for one company long enough to earn a pension. By the time he was in his sixties his sales abilities had waned, and he was forced to move to a cheap rooming house where he lived on a dwindling savings account of a few thousand dollars and a small Social Security check.

Then there was the widow of an IBM communications engineer who had wanted to make a million dollars. He had quit IBM and put his talents and money into marketing communications devices which he designed and manufactured. He had acquired three small companies, but slumping sales forced all three into bankruptcy. This engineer, then in his late fifties, had lacked the foresight to secure his own future; he had neither pension nor solid investments to fall back on. Despondent over his failure, he became an alcoholic and died a few years later, leaving behind a penniless wife.

These stories of people falling from high to low estate are the most dramatic aspects of the retirement threat. However, there are other disasters retirees face that are easier to escape than financial problems. These include feelings of isolation, alienation, and the attendant loneliness and depression; failing health, not necessarily the result of accident, disease, or aging, but the inevitable consequence of not maintaining good health as best you can throughout your life; and an abiding but false sense of powerlessness, the feeling that you can't change the way things are. These problems, and what you can do about them, will also be covered in this book.

THE BIRTH OF A
SENIOR ACTIVIST

These experiences in my community very quickly led me into a second career as a senior activist. I began by helping the people I met. I fixed one lady's leaking faucets and replaced broken boards on another lady's porch. In looking after one person, I'd find two or three others who needed help just as badly. But the more time I spent helping these senior citizens, the more I realized that the problem of poverty among the retired in that community and elsewhere was so pervasive that to have any effect at all, it would have to be attacked on a broader, systematic basis.

I approached the city council of Thousand Oaks, the city I live near, and pleaded with them to allocate funds and services to help the poor retired. They told me it was a federal problem with Social Security and welfare, not the city government's concern. The Ventura County officials gave me the same kind of answer. I finally asked the county to hire me, explaining that I would use my years of business experience, combined with county government resources, to alleviate some of the problem. I was told there were no funds available, and besides I was too old to be a county employee.

I may have been old, but I was persistent. I went to all nine city councils within my county, as well as to the board of supervisors that governs the county and pleaded the cause of the poor retired. Finally, six months after I began getting interested in the problems of the poor retired, I got lucky. The federal government informed the state it had to survey the requirements of its senior citizens in order to be eligible for available federal money to alleviate those needs. The state, in turn, told Ventura County to create and fill the job of senior citizens coordinator to determine those needs. The county hired me.

RETIREMENT POVERTY— NO CLASS BOUNDARIES

My first job as senior citizens coordinator was to identify every senior in the county and find out what his or her needs were. In gathering this information I found that retirement poverty was much more extensive than I had imagined. It knew no class boundaries. It wasn't just working-class or middle-class people who slipped into poverty when they retired. Even some in the upper middle-class—people who had once earned $40,000 a year or more—found themselves traveling the same downward path.

All shared one common failing: they had failed to recognize that retirement would assault their ability to maintain their standard of living, and they had failed to make financial provisions to blunt that assault.

Throughout the years I've seen strangers, friends, and colleagues—formerly comfortable, successful, and sometimes prominent people—sink into the poverty of retirement that I was fortunate enough to avoid. My aim in writing this book, then, is to teach you, too, how to protect yourself against this disaster.

I have tried to avoid too many statistics and tables, which tend to discourage even the heartiest of readers. I do have some charts and some figures when they are essential to illustrate the points that are being made.

If you are familiar with the expression, "There are lies, damn lies, and statistics," you might be tempted to say that I have selected figures that prove my points. To some degree, of course, you would be right. Frequently, two experts dealing with the very same raw material will come up with divergent statistical statements. For instance, in Chapter 3, there is a cost-of-living retirement chart. In a footnote, I indicate that on the average Medicare will pay 38 percent of the $2,500 a year medical care bill which the federal government figures for the average couple over sixty-five. Some statisticians quote this figure at 50 percent which would make my figures a little less frightening—but not a hell of a lot. In general, I have not chosen the most optimistic figure to present to you because it is just this kind of false optimism that I wish to dispel. It is far preferable to be surprised by good news than by bad, and it is the purpose of this book to help you avoid the bad news of the retired life.

I don't pretend to offer a panacea for all the ills that could visit you in retirement. But the advice in these pages will provide you with an abundance of useful information more realistically presented than you will find in most retirement books. It is advice that has to do with the real problems of your retirement: money, health, productivity, security, even the politics of retirement, because you can still make a great many changes that will benefit you directly.

2 THE GREAT RETIREMENT LIE

The books never say, "Watch out, retirement is a threat to your standard of living."

The stories I've just told are true, yet the facts bear little resemblance to the myths that fill most books on how to plan your retirement. I call these myths the Great Retirement Lie.

The recurring theme of the Great Retirement Lie is that retirement is a glorious time of "leisure"—leisure to pursue hobbies, to take trips you couldn't take during your working years, leisure to dine out in lovely, sun-filled restaurants and vacation at beach resorts, to enjoy comfortable evenings at home listening to records while the steaks are sizzling, leisure to visit your children and bounce the grandkids on your knees.

When I read these things I want to laugh and cry at the same time because I know they are far out of the reach of most retirees. In my experience, retired people use their leisure worrying about how bad things will get next year because they have gotten so much worse since last year. They have no spare cash for hobbies (unless their hobby is looking for a job), for dining out, buying a steak, or going to a beach resort. Instead of spending comfortable evenings at home, many retired people I know literally hide in their homes, immersed in the desolation that poverty has brought them in retirement.

As for traveling and enjoying grandchildren, many retired parents stay away from their children except for infrequent trips when they can afford to appear better off than they are. Their children seldom realize the extent to which retirement has eroded their parents' standard of living.

The books never tell you that in retirement most of society regards you as a useless person, a drain on the community and its resources.

The books never say, "Watch out. In retirement, the power that you are used to exercising, however small that may be, is often stripped from you totally."

Some retirement books do allude to poverty, implying that people won't *need* (they avoid the words "won't have") as much money in retirement as they did when working. According to *The Retirement Handbook,* one of the books most frequently reprinted: "You can cut down on 'front' expenses. There is no good reason now for belonging to expensive clubs, owning a costly automobile, wearing expensive clothes, giving parties to impress people." The book also suggests you could cut down by moving to a cheaper neighborhood. It doesn't suggest what to do if you can't cut down on these expenses since you already don't live in an expensive neighborhood or belong to expensive clubs, and so on.

Another retirement book, *Aging Is Not for Sissies*, faces the issue of poverty this way:

> Suppose you are poor. Suppose you don't have investments, insurance, pensions, bank accounts, charge plates, credit cards, and all the rest. . . . When I begin to feel poor I usually go and buy something extrav-

agant—like the time I didn't have enough for the week's food, and I went out and bought six French china plates—Quimpères, they were called. . . . It took away that dreary feeling of just not having enough. Now every time I look at those hand-painted plates, I feel good.

Great practical advice, isn't it?

The most serious fault of many retirement books, however, isn't what they say. It's what they fail to say. They fail to address the most essential element of retirement planning—that of having enough money to maintain a reasonable standard of living. It is part of the Great Retirement Lie to say that you will need less money in retirement to maintain your preretirement standard of living. The truth, however, is that in retirement you can expect to spend almost as much in order to live as you did while employed and getting a full salary. There is very little room for belt-tightening in retirement. People's desires don't change simply because they have stopped working.

As a preview of how retirement may affect your standard of living, why not try the "retirement experiment" devised by syndicated newspaper columnist Lou Cottin. If you have already retired, I'm sure his experiences will come as no surprise to you.

A few years before he quit work, Cottin began a three-month retirement experiment with his wife. Cottin estimated his retirement income would be $1,325 for the three-month period and vowed to live on it no matter what. He wanted to create an accurate portrayal of what retirement would be like for himself and his wife. After he retired, he reported the findings of what he called EXPO—"Our Own Experiment in Poverty"—in his column of May 1976.

FROM SCOTCH AND STEAKS
TO CRACKERS AND CHEESE

A sneak preview of your retirement.

Cottin and his wife had fun with their experiment . . . at first. "We vied with each other in economies," he reported. "My wife would say, 'I picked up a big bag of sawdust free at the lumber yard for the garden bed. Saves us $3.50 on peat moss.' I'd declare, 'I've sworn off beer . . . saves a buck fifty a week.' "

During the second week their twenty-year-old refrigerator broke down—an unexpected expenditure. During the fifth week, Cottin cracked his upper denture, another unexpected expense. And their experiment was only half over.

Then came Father's Day. Cottin's son called to say, "Mom, we'll get home Friday night. Season up the steaks. Check the supply of Scotch. I'm bringing the wine. Sis has cookies. Get tickets for *Fiddler on the Roof*. This'll be a party."

When Cottin's first flush of delight passed, he asked himself, "Who pays the bill?" Right there, the difference between living on retirement income and regular income was forcefully driven home.

"The relationship between parents and children changes," Cottin discovered. "Before, it was Pop and Mom who paid for the family parties and lots more. Now we could no longer pay. Entertainment was out of the question on a retirement income. If they wanted steak, Scotch, and theater tickets, they would have to treat us, and maybe *we'd* supply the wine and cookies . . . .

"When we actually had to live on retirement income, everybody would have to be told 'We're poor' . . . . Not only our children, but we'd also have to proclaim our poverty to good friends whose generous hospitality we had shared and returned, to the good causes to which we'd given freely and cheerfully, to the people in trouble who could count on us for a loan."

For the Cottins and other middle-class families, retirement does not come easily. It is a sharp change, a new way of life demanding tight and thrifty cuts and alterations. Now with the actual experience of a few years of retirement behind him, Cottin concluded: "Yes, our children, our friends, our relatives still visit us, not for dinner, of course. Conversation, we find, goes just as well with crackers and cheese. Everyone knows we can't afford more." Cottin had experienced some of the realities about retirement today.

When you finally decide to stop working, let me suggest that you go into retirement prepared for a siege. Since your credit may end abruptly because you are no longer working, making it much more difficult to take out loans to replace a car or make major repairs on your house, do that buying and repairing while you can, while you still have a job. And give the same attention to yourself and your spouse. If you are covered by medical and dental plans get all the work done before that insurance coverage is stripped from you.

You may think you are safe if you only follow one or two of the suggestions in this book. That's not what I'm proposing. This is not a grab bag of handy alternatives. Every element of retirement that I discuss—financial, work, health, involvement, advocacy—should figure into your planning to some degree.

THE FACTS ABOUT RETIREMENT

Retired persons are the fastest-growing poverty group in the United States.

Many books that sell the Great Retirement Lie read like compilations of government statistics about the financial needs of the retired and Chamber of Commerce handouts glorifying "retirement communities," suggesting where you should buy your retirement home.

Now let's look at some facts about retirement.

Government statistics show that one out of every six seniors lives in poverty. Compare this to one out of every ten for all other age groups. The average income of persons age sixty-five and over in 1975 was $4,800, compared with $12,400 for those eighteen to sixty-four years of age.

Why the difference? According to Dr. Robert Butler, the 1975 Pulitzer Prize-winning author of *Why Survive? Being Old in America,* many of the retired poor became poor only after they retired.

Retired persons also comprise the fastest-growing poverty group in the United States. While poverty among people under sixty-five is steadily declining, poverty among retired people is steadily increasing, and the gap is widening. Statistics indicate that things will get worse before they get better.

In 1969 the U.S. Senate Special Committee on Aging reported that the number of aged poor increased 200,000 from the previous year, while the number of poor in other age groups declined by 1.2 million. In 1975 the Census Bureau reported that 1.3 million Americans—most of them elderly—had slipped into poverty since the previous year.

For the elderly among minority races, the situation is even worse. The government estimates that these people run twice as great a risk of becoming poor as elderly whites. In 1971 the Senate Committee on Aging reported that seven out of ten elderly black Americans had an income below $3,000 a year. Almost half of elderly black women had incomes under $1,000 a year.

This lack of adequate income results in poor health and nutrition. This point was sharply brought home in 1975 by Dr. Jean Mayer, professor of nutrition at Harvard University in Cambridge, Massachusetts, who revealed that many senior citizens subsist on tea, toast, and jelly and that they are "the only segment of our population that gains weight on an ordinary hospital diet." California Governor Jerry Brown told voters in 1974 that 30 percent of the dog food sold in Los Angeles County was consumed by senior citizens.

According to Dr. Butler: "Over half of our elderly population live in deprivation. I am not speaking of lacking money enough to visit one's grandchildren, keep chilled drinks in the refrigerator, or buy a subscription to the local newspaper. I mean lacking food, essential drugs, a telephone in the house to call for help in emergencies." In fact, despite Medicare, more than 50 percent of the elderly cannot even afford to visit their doctors. And one out of three lives in substandard housing.

One of the elements that makes these facts surprising is that the retired poor are not as visible as the younger poor. They are generally not seen loitering on street corners, milling about city parks with "help wanted" sections of the newspaper under their arms, or standing in line for welfare or unemployment checks.

Most of the retired poor stay home, going out only to take their Social Security checks from the mailbox to the bank or to buy groceries from the little "mom and pop" stores down the street. They stay home, afraid of the world, of muggers, of neighbors' stares. And when they overcome those fears and want to go out, many of the retired—especially retired widows—have to rely on public transportation, which is often either too far from their door or too expensive for them to use.

THE RETIREMENT THREAT TO
THE MIDDLE CLASS

The lower-middle classes aren't the only ones who retire into trouble.

Retirement can be much more of a shock for the middle and upper-middle classes than for the very rich or poor. The very rich have resources to battle inflation, which usually robs the retired of buying power, and the poor have spent their whole lifetime managing on tight budgets. But people in the middle and upper-middle classes have limited resources to cope with the runaway cost of living. It is their standard of living that is apt to slip, and this can be most upsetting.

I ran into many depressing examples of this.

A sixty-nine-year-old former oil company geologist, retired since 1953, thought he and his wife had it made when they paid off the mortgage of their handsome, tile-roofed stucco home in Alamo, California. That was before inflation caught up with them. In 1973 their home was assessed for tax purposes at $55,980, which obligated the geologist to pay property taxes of $1,830. By 1975 inflation helped push the assessed valuation to $122,000, which boosted their property taxes to $3,791.

The geologist said, "I just can't afford to pay my taxes. . . . I'm sick about it. I'll have to get work somewhere or give up everything. That's not easy at my age. Twice now I've been put out of jobs on mandatory age restrictions. I just hope I can find something at around $2.50 an hour somehow. My wife and I are at our wits' end. Neither of us has had a solid night's sleep in four months."

Another man, in his seventies, came to me and almost wept when he told me he had reached the lowest point in his life: "It tears me apart to ask this, Mr. Lamb, but I need some help. I'm not as poor as a lot of the people you deal with but I'm just as desperate. I've had too good a life to have it fall apart this way."

He didn't look terribly poor. His clothes were a bit out of style and slightly worn now but had once been fine and obviously made from expensive cloth. He was a handsome, robust man, and I could sense the vitality that still remained in his strong frame.

He told me he had been married to his wife for more than fifty years. "I've always taken good care of her," he said, "but I've reached the point where I can't take care of her anymore."

He had once owned a couple of hardware stores that he had built up from nothing into prosperous businesses. "For more than thirty years," he said, "I could buy my wife and myself new cars every few years, and I would give her all the clothes and dinners out she ever wanted. She never had to worry about money."

Then he sold his stores, made a down payment on a plush $30,000 house trailer, and moved to California to enjoy the rewards of success in retirement. He had started out with nearly $70,000 in a regular savings account and figured he had nothing to worry about.

That was before one sour investment and the bills for a major illness chopped off several thousand dollars in savings, and before inflation began to take giant leaps ahead of the interest rates on his savings accounts. Despite Medicare (which paid for only part of the medical costs), within a few years his savings had nearly vanished. He and his wife had been struck down financially, as if out of nowhere. For the first time in his life he worried about having enough money to pay a bill—the mortgage payment on his mobile home. By the time he came to see me he was also having trouble paying the rental fee on his trailer space as well. Their situation was not crucial in the sense that he and his wife lacked food or medicine to ward off hunger and illness. But the man had reached the point where he couldn't give his wife things he thought she needed.

"Mr. Lamb," he said "I'm seventy-four years old. I've worked hard all my life, and I've been successful. I'm a traditional kind of self-reliant man. I've never asked anything of anyone in my whole life. But now I can't even buy my wife a pair of shoes or any new clothes. And that's not all. Every month I can buy less with what money I do have, and I have to squeeze even more to meet the trailer payment."

I had to tell this man the harsh truth, that he would probably never be able to retain the standard of living he had enjoyed for twenty years. I never told him that things would probably get worse, and that he would eventually lose his trailer to inflation. He had enough to worry about.

The newspaper columnist, geologist, the hardware store owner—all these people are as much the rule as the exception. Their fall from comfort to poverty was a total surprise to them, but it's no surprise to people who know the full retirement scene.

WIDOWHOOD AND THE RETIREMENT THREAT

Most retired widows live in, or close to, poverty.

Women, especially the widows of retired men, have it the toughest. Statistics reveal that 85 percent of retired husbands die before their wives, often leaving the woman without enough money to survive. In many cases the working husband neglected to provide for his wife's support in the event of his death. And if the couple were relying on the husband's pension, what they failed to realize was that the pension might be cancelled upon the husband's death, since a great many pension plans do not provide benefits for survivors.

The result is devastating for older women. According to Tish Sommers, head of the National Organization for Women's (NOW) Task Force on Older Women: "Of those women over sixty-five, 47 percent have incomes of less than $2,000 per year, and only 12 percent receive $5,000 per year or more."

The following story is not unusual. A woman I met, now in her early sixties, had once lived in an expensive home with memberships in nice country clubs. When I first met her on one of my walks around Ventura County, she was sitting in a broken-down old car, weeping. She had only a few dollars in her pocket, and her only income was a monthly $235 welfare check.

Her husband had earned over $40,000 a year as an executive for an electronics firm before he suddenly contracted cancer and was forced to retire. He had always been a climber on the executive ladder and had changed companies whenever a better opportunity presented itself. As a result, he had never remained with one company long enough to earn a pension or acquire a sound medical insurance policy nor had he ever invested in anything but status symbols.

The husband's cancer operation and a long convalescence consumed most of their savings, which had amounted to some $70,000. When the husband died, his widow was compelled to file for bankruptcy to pay off the remaining medical bills. Creditors eventually foreclosed on her home to satisfy the debts. For the rest of her life she would have to resort to welfare and live in cheap rooming houses.

This seemingly melodramatic story is real-life drama, reflecting the retirement predicament of thousands of widows. Is it any wonder that those who deal with the retired so frequently hear the death wish expressed and so often find it fulfilled? Statistics bear this out. The suicide rates among the present generation of retired people, in which men are the prime support of their families, show that about 25 percent of all reported suicides occur in the over-sixty-five population. This accounts for about 11 percent of the total population in this country. According to the U.S. Public Health Service, in 1967 the incidence of suicide among men between fifty-five and sixty-four was twice that of men between twenty-five and thirty-four. The highest incidence of suicides took place among older white men, no doubt because they suffered the greatest fall from prosperity. The increase in suicides among women of the same age groups was 52 percent.

And no wonder, for women are often left with little hope and great despair. A widow once called me at my office and asked if I could provide her with a "kill pill." I asked her what that was. "You know," she said, "something I can take at night so I won't wake up in the morning."

When I tried to dissuade her, she told me angrily that she had as much right to die as she had to live. "They give a horse a quick shot in the head when it's no good to anyone anymore, don't they?" she cried and hung up. That was a woman who hung up too fast for me to help.

Another older widow through sobs told me that she had been the wife of a well-to-do man who died shortly after retirement, leaving her with very little financial resources.

> I never thought I would need you, but I'm at the lowest ebb of my whole life. I'm without food; I have nothing left but coffee. My Social Security check is two weeks overdue. They guaranteed it would come today, but the mailman just left, and when I asked him if he forgot my check, he said he didn't know anything about it. Now I'm going into the weekend with nothing to eat. I wanted to tell you, Mr. Lamb, because you said you wanted to know stories like this so you could know what to do for us old people. I'm going to commit suicide as soon as I hang up. I wanted you to know why.

I called on some volunteers who gave her two days' worth of groceries to get her through the weekend, and on Monday I took her to the local welfare office where she got a partial check.

It was the type of cry I hear often. People who have never experienced poverty before suddenly find themselves with no heat on a cold night or face to face with starvation or no medicine or medical aid when they fall ill.

Because this woman had the good sense to know where to call for help, I was able to talk her into finding other ways to cope with her emergency. But she could have been spared this ordeal had she or her husband thought about the future before it became the present. A pension plan with survival benefits, investments in annuities, or other guaranteed sources of retirement income would have left her comfortable instead of desperate. And other aids could have provided her with a sense of well-being.

To add to the dilemma of widows is the fact that many have never learned how to handle finances and are sometimes at the mercy of less than honest or capable advisors. They've never learned to drive a car and are stranded at home. They fail to make new acquaintances and friends and find themselves more and more set apart from the flow of life.

If these stories have scared the hell out of you—or at least made you stop and think and want to plan ahead—that's what they were intended to do. Retirement more often holds economic disaster and tragedy rather than the green fairways of golf courses, "golden years" retirement cruises, and Norman Rockwell-style family reunions.

But enough. You have the picture, and it isn't rosy. But it need not be black. There are things you can do to start planning now to avoid predicaments as those you've been reading about, to help make retirement not a financial threat or trap but, as it should be, a reward for a productive life.

3 YOUR RETIREMENT BUDGET: How Much Will You Need to Live On?

Neither the government, the financial experts, nor Tony Lamb can do your planning for you.

Most people I meet know only half of what they should know to go into retirement. This ignorance is spread across all social and economic classes.

An example of this was given in an article in the *Wall Street Journal* early in 1977 dealing with how executives handle their money. It quoted three bank officials who specialize as financial counselors. One said that fewer than 25 percent of the executives he sees have systematic savings plans. Another stated that in 20 percent of the interviews he conducted either husband or wife lacked a will. A third counselor reported that "Even among the fifty-year-old executives, fewer than a third have any real idea of how they will finance their retirement." The counselors also commented on such oversights as poorly planned insurance, the failure of people who move from one state to another to revise their wills in accordance with different state laws, and so forth. All of them found one fundamental flaw time after time: a lack of coherent planning to survive the onslaught of retirement and the other tribulations of growing old.

Let me give you another example. Occasionally, I give seminars on retirement planning to middle-aged Navy scientists in Port Hueneme, California—a fairly representative group of middle-class people, a group accustomed to thinking, planning, testing. The main point I try to get across is this: that their pensions will probably not be enough to live on when they retire. And I try to scare them into awareness, actually into action, with the same true-to-life accounts I've already told you. As always, my objective is to wake people up to the urgency of planning now—well before they retire—and not only to plan but to act.

The lack of realistic thinking among these educated people never fails to astonish me. When I flatly announce they will have retirement income problems, someone will stand up and protest that he is going to get $800 a month in retirement and that the Navy told him that that would be plenty to live on. (These prospective retirees' benefits generally fit into a certain category: their retirement pensions will equal half their final salary.) The man is stunned when I tell him the Navy doesn't know what it's talking about.

Here are some of the things I bring up that these men— and the Navy—have not considered. I ask the group if they have been putting half of their working salaries into savings accounts. When they say no, I ask what they intend to give up in retirement. Of course, they don't expect to give up anything. So when I question them about their anticipated retirement expenses, they tell me what the Navy has told them: they won't be buying many of the things which they now need while working full time. The list includes new work clothes, regular haircuts, shoeshines, lunches, contributions to office collections, subscriptions to scientific journals, and gasoline to drive their cars to work. The total amounts to peanuts! A couple of hundred dollars at most.

I tell these men, just as I tell other groups of midde-class prospective retirees, that when they retire they will want to take up or do more of the other things they don't have time for now, like golf, photography, entertaining, or travel. What money they might save on gasoline driving to work they may want to spend traveling to the beach or the mountains. I tell them that when they retire, if they've got the money, they'll undoubtedly end up spending more on gasoline and dining out than they are now spending, since one of the joys of retirement is time to do all these things. I point out that whatever they may give up, they'll want to spend more in some other way, if they have the money. If they continue thinking as they have, they will end up living only half the lives they are living now. And I ask them if that's what they want to do.

ILLUSION VERSUS REALITY: WHAT YOU'LL NEED TO LIVE ON IN RETIREMENT

How expert are the "experts"?

Unrealistic thinking about money is part of the myth that forms the basis of the Great Retirement Lie. Financial "experts" in government and private business generally claim you'll only be spending 75 percent of your preretirement net income to maintain your standard of living in retirement. They give the usual reasons—you can expect to pay less for food, housing, transportation, personal care, recreation, gifts, and just about everything else. But the experts are dead wrong.

If you want to maintain your present standard of living in retirement, you'll spend roughly as much money as you do now. The only adjustments you'll make are upwards—to account for increases in the cost of living.

Now to see what a comfortable standard of living consists of, let's take a look at a typical proposed retirement budget reprinted from a national financial magazine for a couple contemplating retirement in 1980 (Table I). The cost-of-living figures reported in the magazine are based on data from the Bureau of Labor Statistics and have been adjusted to allow for inflation through 1980. I have compared their figures to my own estimates for the same items (Table II).

The magazine's estimate doesn't yield a bad retirement balance sheet—a *surplus* of $100.92 a month, which is $1,211 a year. My own figures are not so optimistic—a deficit of $329.50 a month, or $3,954 a year. Cut it in half, and you've still got a substantial deficit situation.

TABLE I. A TYPICAL MAGAZINE BUDGET FOR A RETIRED COUPLE IN 1980

Income in retirement, per month		Cost of living in retirement, per month	
Social Security	$467.50	Food	$155.00
Veterans' benefits		Housing	203.59
Pensions	55.00	Transportation	52.15
Annuities	50.00	Clothing	33.75
Dividends	7.00	Personal care	17.25
Interest	25.00	Medical care	50.67
Real estate		Recreation, misc.	31.42
Insurance		Taxes:	25.00
Commissions		Local	
Salary or wages	100.00	State	
Other		Federal	
		Other spending:	34.75
Total monthly		Contributions, gifts	
retirement income	**$704.50**	Insurance	
		Savings	
		Long-term debt	
		Other	
		Total monthly	
		retirement budget	**$603.58**
Retirement balance sheet:			
Income		$704.50	
Living costs		603.58	
Surplus		**$100.92**	

At first glance, my cost-of-living figures may seem a bit high because they differ so drastically from the magazine's estimates. But they are not. My figures, in fact, are modest. Living costs of $1,034 a month equal only $12,408 a year.

But don't simply accept as truth the retirement projections propagated in newspapers, magazines, and government

TABLE II. TONY LAMB'S FIGURES FOR THE SAME RETIRED COUPLE IN 1980

Cost of living in retirement, per month	
Food	$200.00
Housing	325.00
Transportation	95.00
Clothing	75.00
Personal care	40.00
Medical care	129.00*
Recreation, misc.	50.00
Taxes:	70.00
Local	
State	
Federal	
Other spending:	50.00
Contributions, gifts	
Insurance	
Savings	
Long-term debt	
Other	
Total monthly retirement budget	$1,034.00
Income in retirement, per month (from Table I)	$704.50†
Retirement balance sheet:	
Income	$704.50
Living costs	1,034.00
Deficit	$329.50

*The federal government reports that, on the average, a person 65 and over spends $1,250 a year for medical care, which is $2,500 for a couple. On the average, Medicare will pay 38 percent of that amount, leaving a balance of $1,550, or $129 a month.

†I'm using the magazine's estimated monthly retirement income since the amount appears reasonable for a couple who have failed to plan adequately for their retirement years.

publications. Don't accept my figures either. Examine your own life. Decide whether so-called retirement experts really know what they're talking about, and then do your own planning and figuring.

For instance, do you think that you'll be spending only $155 a month for food by 1980 as the magazine's budget specifies? Why, according to the U.S. Department of Commerce, in 1974 a retired couple living on a "moderate budget" was already spending $123 a month. Even if you take figures from the government's own Consumer Price Index (which shows the year-to-year rise in the cost of food as well as other items), you'll find that food costs rose over 58 percent in the six years prior to 1974. Why shouldn't we assume they will rise by that much in the six years after 1974? (Two years later, at the end of 1976, the cost of living had already increased 20 percent.) I've done the arithmetic for you in my own chart. As you can see, my figures project that the average retired person will spend $194 (rounded to $200 for inflation) per month for food by 1980.

Where did the magazine get its $155 figure? Perhaps a little more figuring will give us a clue.

I based my food cost projections on a retired couple living on a "moderate budget," a budget that ensures essentials. But the Department of Commerce gives 1974 food cost figures of $96.63 a month for a retired couple living on a "low budget"—that is, a poor person's budget. Using the same 58 percent-plus projected increase in food costs for the next six years, that retired poor couple can expect to pay $152.77 per month for food by 1980, which is remarkably close to the magazine's estimate. Obviously, the magazine's budget is projecting that retired people will eat like poor people. And that's exactly how you will be eating if you fall for such typically unrealistic cost projections.

Now let's go an important step further. I said I based my 1980 food cost figure on a "moderate budget." But the Census Bureau says that if you have an income of $22,937 a year you are not living moderately, but are among the highest-earning 20 percent of the American population. So, if your earnings are near that figure and you would like to maintain your present standard of living when you retire, you should be estimating your food cost budget on the Commerce Department's "liberal budget" figures. The "liberal food budget" for a retired couple in 1974 was $143.43 a month. Projecting forward with the same 58 percent cost-of-living increase that we have been using, this typical upper-middle-class retired couple can expect to pay $227 per month for food in 1980. I projected only $200.

In summary, the magazine's projected food budget for a retired couple in 1980 is for a poor couple. My estimate is for a couple who can afford essentials—like a balanced meal. But if you are used to more than the essentials—if you are used to having dinner in a restaurant once a week or now and then enjoying a choice cut of steak—then your 1980 food budget should be estimated at the higher, "liberal budget" level.

However you look at it, the magazine's budget is too low by far for any couple to maintain a comfortable standard of living in retirement.

A FEW MORE EXAMPLES OF
FAULTY REASONING

Figure it up for yourself.

The magazine's budget is typical of the "advice" given by other experts to those contemplating retirement. And it is just this kind of purported advice that is responsible for retirement poverty—indirectly, at least.

Let me briefly examine a few more examples of the faulty reasoning in the Great Retirement Lie, this time using just plain common sense to see how dangerously inadequate the figures are.

Housing Costs

The magazine suggests your housing will cost $203.59 a month in 1980. That is simply ludicrous. By 1980 who can seriously entertain the notion of paying only $203 a month to live in an apartment or paying that much mortgage on a house? Since 1972 housing costs have risen 15 percent each year. By the end of the decade you'll be lucky to find any place to live for $325 a month.

Personal Care

This figure of $17.25 a month for personal care is sadly inadequate. If the couple were to get the cheapest of hair-cuts and beauty salon attention that sum would almost be spent. Not only that, but isn't the retired couple of 1980 to buy toothpaste, toilet paper, soap, shampoo, razor blades, deodorant, cosmetics? Are these the items retired people are expected to give up in order to live cheaper than working people?

Medical Care

The budget in the magazine says a retired couple will need $50.67 per month in 1980 for medical care. That estimate is not only ridiculous, it's dangerous. My figure of $129 a month is for 1976. In 1974 medical costs rose 13 percent over the previous year; in 1975 they rose 16 percent. If that trend continues, by 1980 the $129 figure will turn into $200. And it could go even higher.

Birthdays and Christmas

You'll notice the magazine's budget doesn't account for contributions and gifts. Perhaps they expect you to stop giving birthday or holiday presents to your children or grandchildren and anniversary gifts to your spouse.

Insurance

The magazine makes the incredible supposition that you'll need no insurance in retirement, for the article provides no estimate on this expenditure. How can they reasonably believe you would drive a car without insurance or not consider insuring your household belongings against fire or theft? Are retirees expected to go without medical insurance, knowing that they pay three times more medical fees than the preretired?

To summarize, in the last decade the cost of living has risen by more than 70 percent. If the trend continues, which it undoubtedly will, it will go up more than 70 percent in the next ten years. Since the Social Security cost-of-living increase is inadequate and most pensions have no cost-of-living increase, that means for much of that 70 percent increase there will be a corresponding reduction in your retirement income.

When the experts estimate that you will need "a little less" in retirement, they also figure you'll be content to lead a lot less of a life. Nearly all of the proposed retirement budgets I have seen make no provisions for vacations, the experts apparently assuming that retired people don't want to go anywhere. There were minimal allowances for mortgage payments and rents, clothing, and no dining out. And, of course, they never made provisions for such luxuries as an occasional glass of wine or beer, regular games of golf, or veterinary care for pets.

Most of the information disseminated about retirement, both by government and private publications, is misleading. Whatever the motivation, the information is false. It perpetuates the Great Retirement Lie.

These are the facts as I know them and as I have seen them work in the lives of seniors I know. My frankness is an upsetting experience for people, as I hope it will be for you, too. It is not easy to accept, especially if you are in your forties and fifties when earnings are good and retirement seems far down the road.

You might ask me the same question that a young scientist did who had been listening to my stories. "What would you suggest I do so I don't end up in the same fix as these guys?"

I shot back my answer: "Get rich or die young."

"There has to be a better answer than that," he said. And, of course, he was right. There is another answer, but it's not a simple solution.

To begin with, you need to take a look at where your retirement income will be coming from, and you need to understand that some sources you've been counting on (such as pensions, Social Security, savings) may be far from secure—or even adequate—as you will see in the next chapter.

4 SOCIAL SECURITY, PENSIONS, AND SAVINGS: Less Certain Than You Think

Your Social Security (if the system hasn't gone broke), your pension (if you get one), or your savings (after inflation has taken its bite) probably will not be enough.

You may feel that up to now I have unnecessarily frightened you. You might have a pension. Perhaps you are paying into the Social Security system, or if you are over sixty-five you might already be receiving monthly checks. You may even have a healthy savings account. Those bastions you are counting on may be weaker than you think, however. Let's take a look at them more carefully.

SOCIAL SECURITY

How much can you really expect?

The Social Security system was established in 1935 as a retirement insurance program for the retired in industry and

33

commerce. Later, the law was revised to cover the surviving spouse in the event the worker died, and the coverage was extended to include household and farm workers, governmental employees, members of the military, the clergy, and the self-employed. Today the law covers nearly everyone, although nonprofit organizations and most teachers who do not pay into the Social Security system are not covered.

An employee pays a percentage of his or her income to Social Security during working years and, when that person retires, he or she—or a surviving spouse, in case of the worker's death—is paid a monthly cash sum to make up for loss of income in later years when no longer employed. The money paid to the worker or the surviving spouse is, in theory, the money the worker has contributed to the Social Security system during working years. In other words, it is money the worker has earned and put aside through compulsory payments. It is not just a government handout.

Even if you expect to get a pension, your main source of income in retirement in all likelihood may come from these Social Security payments. You are eligible to collect full benefits at sixty-five. If you retire early and begin collecting at sixty-two, your benefits will be cut by 20 percent and will remain at that level for the rest of your life.

Before we go further, let me just say that I think stepping out of the labor force early is tantamount to stepping on a land mine. I have very few good words to say about early retirement, except that the only time you should ever consider it is if you get a much better offer from another company, one that you can't refuse. Not only do I suggest not taking early retirement, I also strongly recommend that you retire only when you are actually forced out.

Once you do retire, you will notice that the amount of Social Security payments changes often. As of this writing, they range from a maximum of $387 a month for a retired individual to a maximum of $580 a month for a retired couple. Sounds good. Unfortunately, payments are generally much lower. The average individual benefit in 1975 was

$206 a month, or $2,472 a year—below the government's 1975 poverty level figure of $2,724.

The amount of the Social Security payment becomes even lower when you calculate the effects of inflation on that sum. Legislation provides automatic cost-of-living increases for Social Security recipients, but they simply are not enough to keep up with inflation. If the cost of living in a calendar year rises 3 percent or more, Social Security recipients are given a corresponding boost in their checks. Unfortunately, the increase does not go into effect until June of the following year in which the cost-of-living increase occurs, so Social Security recipients still don't quite keep up with inflation.

The Bankers Trust of New York conducted a study of 1972 Social Security increases and found that when the cost-of-living adjustments were taken into account, the increases amounted to about 18 percent by the year 1975. The dollar meanwhile slipped in value by 27 percent. The result was a 9 percent loss in Social Security benefits to retired persons.

As inadequate as Social Security payments are for the retired of today, the retired of the future may be lucky if they receive any Social Security payments at all. During the past few years every leading newspaper in the country has carried major articles about the potential bankruptcy of the Social Security system. An editorial in the *Los Angeles Times* in March of 1977 summed it up succinctly: "Barring a cut in benefits or an increase in payroll taxes, Social Security will go broke sometime early in the 1980s. One component, the disability insurance fund, will be out of money by the end of 1979."

These projections are based on some frightening facts. Warren Shore, a consumer advocate who has explored what he views as the imminent demise of the Social Security system in a book entitled *Social Security: The Fraud in Your Future*, says that the system has already gone broke and is drawing on general tax revenues to make ends meet.

Congress has seriously mismanaged the system over the years, consistently allocating more Social Security benefits to recipients than the amount of Social Security taxes it levied on the work force. Since the number of retired people grew at a greater rate than the number of working younger people, members of Congress won the votes of the retired by sanctioning higher Social Security payments, but didn't have the nerve to levy new Social Security taxes on the working population, whose votes they also wanted.

The trick was being played on retired people of the future. Now the fund has been largely depleted, and the current work force is not big enough to replenish the fund for present and future payments without its having to pay whopping new taxes.

Another reason the Social Security system has run out of money is due to the rapid growth of the retirement population during this century. In 1900, persons over sixty-five accounted for only 4 percent of the population; at present, they account for 12 percent. And by the year 2000, the senior population will account for more than 20 percent of the total population. People are living longer and are being retired earlier. In 1900, people over age sixty-five made up 36 percent of the work force. In 1976, this percentage dropped to 14 percent. The decline for men also has been steady, from 63 percent in 1900 to 21 percent in 1976. The female rate remained the same, at about 8 percent.

Compulsory retirement policies, in which companies force their employees to quit at age sixty-five, affect 50 percent of all American workers. According to one expert, "Given present tendencies, Americans may soon spend up to one-third of their lives in retirement." Plug that surge in the retirement population into the Social Security system, and you will find that although in 1947 only one out of every seventy-one Americans was getting Social Security benefits, in 1975 one out of every seven Americans was receiving payments.

Where will the money come from? Warren Shore says: "In 1955 seven U.S. workers paid taxes for every person collecting benefits. Today fewer than three workers 'pool' their 'contributions' for each Social Security beneficiary. By early next century only two Americans will be working for every one collecting a [Social Security] check."

How can the Social Security system survive under these conditions? What is not, of course; a tenable solution is to increase taxes to the point where every two workers support one retired person. By the time the worker pays his Social Security, his income tax, and has the remaining taxes deducted from his paycheck, he will have less than half his salary left. The next generation of taxpayers is not likely to stand for that.

Will the system go bankrupt? That is certainly a possibility. Other large institutions have. In 1975 New York City would have gone bankrupt if the federal government had not stepped in to bail it out with enormous loans. It was in trouble again in early 1977. Other cities, municipalities, and counties all over the country have experienced the crunch. Tomorrow is not apt to be better than today.

My own view is that the Social Security system in this country will continue to operate because it has to. The government cannot allow large segments of the population to starve because they have no income. But there will unquestionably be loud public demands to curtail the runaway cost of the system. So if you are counting on Social Security as your prime source of income, don't expect a very comfortable retirement. It is improbable that the benefits will increase in the future as they have during the last decade.

PENSIONS: A TRICKY BUSINESS

Will you get a pension? And will it be enough?

The earliest pension plans were entirely in the hands of the employing companies, who gave a small amount of money a month—certainly not enough to live on—to a few long-term employees as a reward for dedicated service. At the time, there were no unions or organized labor groups which could demand anything more for the retiring worker. As labor organized, pensions gradually became part of the wages and fringe benefits that unions negotiated with employers for their members. But employers continued to regard pensions as gratuities they gave to employees rather than as part of the overall wage package they have become, and unions were more concerned with immediate wage hikes than they were with the fringe benefits, such as pensions.

Historically, company pensions have represented one of the greatest frauds ever perpetrated upon the American worker. Although more than half of our country's workers are covered by some form of company pension, most have either not collected their pensions or have received a much smaller one than promised. Workers have been led to believe that their company pension will see them through their retirement years in style, but the cold fact is that private and public pensions account for only about 12 percent of the income of persons age sixty-five and over.

As Ralph Nader told the Sixth Annual Conference on Employee Benefits in 1972: "At least one-half of all persons participating in private pension plans will not receive pension benefits when they retire." Senator Jacob Javits, a pioneer in the battle for pension reform, estimated that as few as one of every twelve workers ever actually collects his pension.

This was because until early 1974, when protective legislation was enacted, employees' chances for receiving pension benefits were minimal because of bankruptcy of the companies they worked for as well as mismanagement of funds.

Bankruptcy is exemplified by the Studebaker Corporation's South Bend, Indiana, factory closing down in 1963. Its 4,000 workers, some of whom had worked for the company for forty years, discovered there was little money

left in their pension fund. Many of the workers received
nothing; others received 15 percent of what they had been
promised. They are not alone. Approximately 30,000 workers a year lose out on company pensions because of
bankruptcy.

The problem of mismanagement was demonstrated in
1970 when it was revealed that $75 million of the United
Mine Workers Welfare and Retirement Fund was deposited
in the National Bank of Washington, where it drew no
interest. The money, which accounted for 44 percent of the
union's pension fund, could have earned $12 million in
interest had it been invested in interest-drawing stocks and
bonds.

When investigations into such incidents revealed how
extensive this problem was, some thought was given to
eliminating the causes. It began in 1971 when a congressional committee examined eighty-seven pension plans
where there were indications that workers were not getting
their pensions. The committee found that in fifty-one of the
plans, only 5 percent of the active participants ever collected any money. In the other thirty-six plans, 16 percent
collected.

So in 1974, Congress enacted pension reform legislation,
known as the Employee Retirement Income Security Act,
which was the first major federal attempt to regulate private
pensions. (Some provisions of the law are detailed in the
next chapter, but for more complete information you may
be interested in a $7 publication explaining the law available
from Commerce Clearing House in Los Angeles, San Francisco, and Chicago. Specify that you want material on IRS
rules for pensions.)

This act attempts to guarantee workers their pensions
under many formerly unprotected circumstances. The new
law has not yet been adequately tested, so it is still a matter
of conjecture as to how effective it will be. Problems still
exist. In 1976, twenty-eight of the thirty top executives of
the Central States Teamsters Pension Fund—the largest of

its kind, with assets of $1.4 billion—were fired after accusations of mismanagement. The Justice Department revealed that millions of dollars of the fund were unaccounted for.

The new law of 1974 is a step in the right direction, though you should be aware that there are still other ways you can lose out on your pension. They're important to know about you so you can prepare your own future more securely.

SIX GOOD REASONS WHY YOU MAY NOT GET YOUR PENSION

Losing it is easier than you think.

You're Not Vested

You may not get a pension if you retire before serving the specified number of years. The American labor force is one of the most mobile in the world, yet most pension plans require that an employee maintain long, continuous service with one company in order to qualify. The requirement, known as *vesting*, generally calls for the employee to log from ten to fifteen years of service with one company. Statistics show that most retiring men have less than fifteen years of service, women less than ten years.

Vesting is vital because without it you receive only that portion of your pension that you have put into the plan. You get nothing of what the employer put into it. If your pension plan is funded entirely by your employer, you get nothing from the plan at all if you leave the company before you are vested. About 75 percent of all private pension plans are funded entirely by employers; most of the remaining plans have employers matching the employees' contributions.

A major problem of acquiring vested interest is that companies have been known to lay off their employees just before they receive the vested interest in their pension. The company simply cites "economic reasons" and lays the employee off to "effect economies." There are numerous documented cases of this where workers were laid off just months prior to reaching their ten-year vesting requirement.

You Change Jobs

You may not get a pension if you leave your present job to take one with another company. Most pensions are not portable, that is, they cannot be transferred from one job to another. If you take another position, in all likelihood you will have to begin all over again to gain a vested interest in the new company's pension plan.

You Get Promoted

You may not get a pension if you receive a promotion within the same company. The pension plan that covered you as a blue-collar worker may not be the plan that covers you as a manager.

You Have Not Worked the Minimum Number of Weeks per Year

You may not get a pension if you do not work the minimum number of weeks per year during the time you fulfill the continuous service requirement. Some plans require, for example, that you work a minimum of thirty-five weeks per year to qualify. If your work weeks are cut back for any reason (sickness, leave of absence) you may be disqualified.

You Take a Job with a Competitor

You may not get a pension if you quit your present job and go to work for a competitor, even though you may have already fulfilled all other requirements. Some pension plans have provisions that forbid employment with a competitor under penalty of losing your "earned" pension rights.

Your Pension Plan Ends

You may not get a pension if the pension plan is terminated through bankruptcy or if the company is sold. This is an area of abuse that has been largely, although not completely, corrected by the 1974 pension reform act. Now the federal government guarantees the "vested" pension benefits.

SURVIVOR'S BENEFITS

The surviving spouse usually gets nothing.

Most workers who are entitled to pensions assume that their spouses will continue to receive pension payments in the event of their own death. Actually, in many plans, the opposite is true—the surviving spouse of a dead pensioner gets nothing. That's one of the reasons why the great majority of widows over sixty-five live at, or below, the poverty level.

Of the plans that do include survivor's benefits, there are three general ways to take a pension, although most retiring couples are unaware of these options. When ready to retire, you can:

1. Take 100 percent of your monthly retirement benefit, in which case your surviving spouse gets nothing after your death.

2. Take 50 percent of your monthly retirement benefit. When you die, your surviving spouse continues to get 50 percent.
3. Take 75 percent of your monthly benefit. When you die, your spouse gets 25 percent.

Now that you are aware of the inadequacy and unreliability of pensions for you and your survivor, where will you look next for income to live on when you stop working?

SAVINGS ACCOUNTS

Most people save at a loss.

After Social Security and pensions, most people depend upon their savings (that is, money in the bank as well as all forms of investments) as the most significant source of financial security for their retirement years. Except for the extremely wealthy, most people in America today know how difficult it is to save money. More and more middle-class and upper-middle-class people enter their forties and fifties with perhaps only their home as an appreciating asset. What savings they have may be going for such preretirement expenses as the education of their children and unexpected increases in property taxes. On top of all these factors that eat away at one's hard-accumulated capital, inflation inexorably increases today's—and the future's—cost of living. For example, if you have budgeted $3,000 a year for a child's education who may be five years away from entering college, you can count on that figure increasing to $4,700 because experts predict college costs will rise by some 58 percent over a five-year period. Like Social Security and your pension, your savings, unless they are truly extraordinary, may not provide you with the security that you are hoping for.

What is to be done? How can you make your way in what may be an increasingly hazardous world? You must prepare yourself. Denying the realities of retirement will not make them disappear. Dealing with them, however—and they can be dealt with—will put you in a stronger position. Let's survey some things that can make up your main bulwarks against a shaky financial retirement.

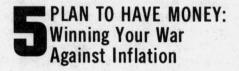5 PLAN TO HAVE MONEY: Winning Your War Against Inflation

---

If you don't understand the effects of inflation, you could end up saving your way into poverty.

A man I know named Ralph retired in 1970 and planned his retirement so he would have $7,000 a year to live on. That was an adequate amount then. It gave him a little over $134 a week, which was higher than the 1970 average wage earner's salary of $119 a week.

But inflation quickly changed that. By 1975 the average weekly wage was $158 a week. By 1980, ten years after Ralph retired, the average weekly wage will be $197. Five years after that it will be $259. But Ralph's weekly retirement income will still be $134 a week.

Ralph is slowly sinking into retirement poverty, for he failed to take inflation into account in his retirement plans. Most authors of books on retirement planning don't consider inflation either. But inflation—the relative decline of the purchasing power of your dollars from year to year—is the most crucial, yet most frequently overlooked, aspect of financial planning.

When you begin figuring your financial future you must project the impact of inflation on your retirement income. Inflation is built into your life, and always will be, since experts believe a small amount of inflation is a healthy economic stimulus. It's debatable whether it's good for the economy, but it's bad for retired people.

For the last twenty-five years this country has been able to hold the rate down, but there's no guarantee it will continue this way. In fact, higher, not lower, inflationary rates are predicted. England's 10 percent year-in and year-out rate of inflation could certainly happen here.

Probably, inflation will only rain on your retirement, not storm on it. But you'd better be prepared. If you have $100,000 in your pocket now, in twenty years it will have the purchasing power of only $38,000. Another way of saying it is that if your present standard of living is based on a $20,000 annual income, in ten years you will have to make $32,600 a year to maintain the same standard. And in twenty years you will need $53,000. And in thirty years you will need $86,400. Working people will achieve increases in their incomes because, historically, salaries have kept abreast or ahead of inflation. But retired people must rely on their retirement funds.

The main financial problem in planning for retirement, obviously, is building up a big enough retirement fund—in the form of pensions, savings, and various investments—to assure yourself of an adequate annual income with a purchasing power that won't be steadily eroded by inflation. If your fund is not set up this way, your standard of living in retirement will steadily decrease each year.

As you will see, inflation remains unchecked in our society and there is a potential for loss of your capital through poor planning or bad luck or unexpected illness.

How, then, can you accumulate enough money for retirement? There is only one way, and that is to save a certain percentage of your salary and invest it at a high enough rate of interest to overcome the erosive effects of inflation. My rule of thumb is that *you invest at least 15 percent of your annual gross income into places that have about an 8 percent growth rate*. Unfortunately, I don't believe that most of the people reading this book will be able to do this. For most of us, this is either impossible or would demand such heavy sacrifices for only potential future benefits that the motivation simply would not be strong enough. However, this does not diminish the desirability of doing it if we can. In fact, the government makes it possible for a self-employed or a pensionless individual to set up a 15 percent tax-deductible retirement plan. I will discuss these major alternatives of investing your money in this chapter.

The fact that you can't do this, however, makes it all the more imperative to pay attention to the next chapter in this book, which shows you how to supplement your income in retirement years. Some of you—in fact, most people over fifty—will have to plan to work in retirement.

Now let's see what you need to do to maintain a reasonable standard of living. Take a few minutes to look at Table I (pp. 48–49). I know tables like this turn readers off. It is just this wariness about tables, charts, and dollars that you, as a prospective retiree, will have to overcome. If you spend a few minutes now to see what your situation really is, you may save yourself years of anguish and distress in unnecessarily impoverished retirement.

Based on your present investment habits, Table I shows you how many years you will be able to maintain your present standard of living after age sixty-five. The table is for people whose annual income is between $15,000 and $30,000, but you can estimate your own category if your income is above or below those points.

Three important assumptions are built into the table. It assumes (1) you are making Social Security payments, (2) your income will go up 5.5 percent a year, and (3) inflation will continue at 5 percent a year. If you are not on Social Security and not getting raises, and if inflation gets even a few percentage points worse, then you can probably count on not sustaining your present standard of living after you retire.

Here's how the table works:

1. Find your age at the left of the table.
2. Place your finger on the second column on the growth rate at which you are (or might be) investing 15 percent of your annual income into your retirement fund.
3. Now move your finger across the table until you arrive under the column that gives your present annual income. Your finger is now resting on the number of years you can expect your retirement fund to maintain your present standard of living after you retire at age sixty-five.

TABLE I. HOW MANY YEARS YOU CAN MAINTAIN YOUR PRESENT STANDARD OF LIVING IN RETIREMENT IF YOU INVEST 15% OF YOUR GROSS INCOME

If you begin investing 15% of your gross income at:	at an annual growth rate of:	then the column below gives the number of years after 65 your retirement fund will maintain your present standard of living if your annual income now is:			
		$15,000	$20,000	$25,000	$30,000
age 40	7%	12	10	9	9
	8%	16	13	12	11
	9%	22	17	15	14
	10%	35	25	21	19
	11%	50+	50+	37	32
	12%	50+	50+	50+	50+
age 45	7%	9	7	7	6
	8%	11	9	8	8
	9%	13	11	10	9
	10%	17	13	12	11
	11%	24	18	15	14
	12%	50+	27	22	20
	13%	50+	50+	50+	36
	14%	50+	50+	50+	50+

If you begin investing 15% of your gross income at:	at an annual growth rate of:	then the column below gives the number of years after 65 your retirement fund will maintain your present standard of living if your annual income now is:			
		$15,000	$20,000	$25,000	$30,000
age 50	7%	6	5	5	4
	8%	7	6	5	5
	9%	8	7	6	6
	10%	9	8	7	6
	11%	11	9	8	7
	12%	14	11	9	9
	13%	18	13	11	11
	14%	29	18	15	13
	15%	50+	30	21	18
	16%	50+	50+	50+	38
age 55	7%	3	3	3	2
	8%	4	3	3	3
	9%	4	3	3	3
	10%	5	4	3	3
	11%	5	4	4	4
	12%	6	5	4	4
	13%	6	5	5	4
	14%	7	6	5	5
	15%	8	7	6	5
	16%	10	8	7	6
age 60	7%	1	1	1	1
	8%	1	1	1	1
	9%	2	1	1	1
	10%	2	1	1	1
	11%	2	1	1	1
	12%	2	1	1	1
	13%	2	2	1	1
	14%	2	2	1	1
	15%	2	2	2	1
	16%	2	2	2	1

To give an example, if you are forty-five and invested 15 percent of your income every year into a retirement fund earning 8 percent, and your present annual salary is $15,000, then your retirement fund would last you eleven years, or until you reached seventy-six. If you are fifty, and your retirement fund were growing at a rate of 10 percent annually, and your present salary is $25,000, your retirement fund would last you seven years after you retired. But as you can see, the older you are when you begin to invest money, the fewer years your retirement fund will last.

If you already have a nest egg saved, you can easily plug it into the table. Table II will show you how. Simply compare your present retirement fund (pensions, savings, investments) to your present annual income. If, as the chart shows, your present retirement fund is three-and-a-half times your annual income, you can see you have a fifteen-year head start toward accumulating your final retirement fund. So when referring to Table I, pretend your age is forty if you are actually fifty-five, and you will find how many years your fund will last in retirement. Similarly, if you are age fifty and have a retirement fund equal to 90 percent of your annual income. move up five years on the table and use the figures for age forty-five.

According to statistics, once age sixty-five is reached a man can expect to live another sixteen years and a woman nineteen. So if you are fifty-five and have not yet begun to invest in some retirement fund and have no accumulated nest egg, you have already run out of time to build up a sufficient amount to maintain your present standard of living during your entire retirement. If this is your sit-uation—and it is the predicament of all too many peo-ple—you may still have enough time to invest in a fund so it will maintain a portion of your present standard of living during retirement.

Table III, patterned after Table I, shows how many years your retirement fund will maintain 80 percent of your present standard of living.

**TABLE II. IF YOU ALREADY HAVE A HEAD START
TOWARD YOUR RETIREMENT FUND**

If you plan to put away 15% of your annual gross income . . .	
and have already accumulated:	move up on Table I
90 percent of a year's income	5 years
2 times present income	10 years
3½ times present income	15 years

TABLE III. HOW MANY YEARS YOU CAN MAINTAIN 80% OF YOUR PRESENT STANDARD OF LIVING IN RETIREMENT IF YOU INVEST 15% OF YOUR GROSS INCOME

If you begin investing 15% of your gross income at:	at an annual growth rate of:	then the column below gives the number of years after 65 your retirement fund will maintain 80% of your present standard of living if your annual income now is:			
		$15,000	$20,000	$25,000	$30,000
age 40	7%	21	16	13	13
	8%	29	21	17	16
	9%	50+	30	24	23
	10%	50+	50+	42	37
	11%	50+	50+	50+	50+
age 45	7%	15	11	10	9
	8%	18	14	12	11
	9%	25	17	15	14
	10%	40	24	19	18
	11%	50+	41	28	26
	12%	50+	50+	50+	50+
age 50	7%	10	7	6	6
	8%	11	9	7	7
	9%	14	10	9	8
	10%	17	12	10	10
	11%	22	15	12	11
	12%	37	19	15	14
	13%	50+	30	21	19
	14%	50+	50+	43	32
	15%	50+	50+	50+	50+
age 55	7%	6	4	4	4
	8%	6	5	4	4
	9%	7	5	5	4
	10%	8	6	5	5
	11%	9	7	6	5
	12%	10	7	6	6
	13%	12	8	7	7
	14%	15	10	8	8
	15%	20	12	9	9
	16%	37	15	11	10
age 60	7%	2	2	1	1
	8%	2	2	2	1
	9%	3	2	2	2
	10%	3	2	2	2
	11%	3	2	2	2
	12%	3	2	2	2
	13%	3	2	2	2
	14%	4	3	2	2
	15%	4	3	2	2
	16%	4	3	2	2

As you can see from the tables, it's not a simple matter to invest money for your retirement. In fact, inflation makes it a formidable task, especially if you are in your mid-fifties. If you are in this age bracket and have not yet accumulated any kind of reserve, it is impossible to build up a sufficient retirement fund to maintain your present standard of living unless you either invest upwards of 50 percent of your income or invest your money in ventures with about a 20-percent growth rate. These are near-impossible goals for most people. So, if you are one of those who do not have enough working years left to build up an adequate retirement fund, my advice is that you invest all the money you can at the highest growth rate available (which we will discuss later in this chapter).

Let's begin by discussing Social Security and company pensions to make sure you actually receive those anticipated retirement staples. Then we'll consider some investment alternatives. There are plenty to choose from. It all depends upon your individual circumstances and desires.

SOCIAL SECURITY

Making sure it's there.

In the previous chapter I pointed out that many experts feel our Social Security system rests on an extraordinarily weak financial base. But despite that weakness there is little reason to fear that Social Security benefits will cease to be paid to the retired in the future. Although the Social Security system may run out of money, the federal government won't, and the federal government is not about to notify 25 million retired voters they will no longer receive the Social Security checks they paid into the system and were promised all their working lives. At present, nine out of ten workers are covered by means of Social Security tax payroll deductions, with the exceptions as noted in the previous chapter. Although Social Security payments are inadequate by themselves (as we've already seen), they are a valuable supplement to your pension and other retirement income.

But since Social Security is an important factor in your retirement picture, be certain you are covered by Social Security by checking with the Social Security Administration, P.O. Box 57, Baltimore, Maryland 21203. If by chance you became a victim of a clerical error in the Social Security system, the Social Security tax you are paying might not be recorded under your Social Security number. Although I hope it need not be, that monthly payment could be your lifeline in retirement.

In addition, you should check to find out if you will have accumulated enough working quarters to be eligible for benefits when you do retire. Here is how this is estimated: you get one quarter of Social Security coverage for each three-month period that you receive wages of $50 or more out of which there were Social Security tax deductions. So a whole calendar year gives you four quarters of coverage. If you are self-employed, you receive four quarters of coverage for each year you net $400 or more profit. But if you are self-employed, remember you must pay your own Social Security taxes; there is no other employer to take it out of your paycheck.

Eligibility

Table IV from the Social Security Administration will help you determine how many quarters you need to be eligible for the maximum amount of Social Security benefits. For example, if you reach age sixty-two in 1981, you must have accrued thirty working quarters, or seven-and-a-half years' full-time work, to be eligible for benefits. Remember, though, that if you begin collecting benefits at age sixty-two when you are first eligible, or at any time before sixty-five, your benefits will be reduced and will remain lower for the rest of your life.

**TABLE IV. SOCIAL SECURITY WORK CREDITS
FOR RETIREMENT BENEFITS**

If you reach 62* in	Quarters you need	Years of full-time work
1977	26	6½
1978	27	6¾
1979	28	7
1981	30	7½
1983	32	8
1987	36	9
1991 or later	40	10

* Age 62 is the earliest you can begin collecting Social Security benefits.

If you want to clarify your position, write to the Social Security Administration at the address given earlier. A special postcard is provided for these purposes at your local Social Security office. Be sure to sign the request and include your age, address, and Social Security number. Ask how many quarters you have accumulated and how many more you need. Also ask how much Social Security tax is being entered in your federal Social Security account, and make sure it compares with the Social Security taxes your employer is deducting from your salary.

Here are a few things you can do if you will not have accrued sufficient working quarters to qualify for maximum benefits for Social Security when the time comes to retire. You could arrange for a friendly employer to hire you with the understanding that you just want to accumulate enough quarters to get Social Security. The employer will really have to be quite friendly, however, because it will cost that person out-of-pocket money above and beyond the deductions in order to help you secure these benefits. Or you could start a business of your own and become self-employed. However, you will have to pay your own self-employment tax to the government (which is the same as Social Security taxes) in order to be eligible for Social Security payments.

Benefits

The amount of your Social Security payments depends on the average of your earnings over a period of years. Of course, the higher your average annual earnings, the bigger your benefit. The method of computing your check is complicated and subject to frequent changes. Once you retire and start receiving your monthly check, make sure you are paid the proper amount. I have found hundreds of people who, through clerical errors, were being short-changed thousands of dollars. If you discover an error, you may have a good deal of retroactive Social Security payments due you. Check with your local Social Security office to make sure you are receiving the right amount. To help you estimate the amount, you might wish to visit one of the 1,300 local Social Security offices across the country and get the free booklet, *Estimating Your Social Security Check*, or write to the Social Security Administration for a copy.

Other benefits are available through the Social Security system: burial payments, aid for underage children, and others. It would be worthwhile finding out what you are entitled to. Additional information on this complex matter may be found in the free booklet, *Your Social Security Rights and Responsibilities.*

A word about government brochures, any government brochure. Government brochures give you the rules and tell you how to play the game. They don't tell you how to win. In order to maximize the potential of their programs, you have to read the material carefully and figure out not only what the government specifically allows you to do, which is clearly stated, but, more importantly, what the government doesn't prohibit you from doing.

Supplemental Security Income (SSI)

Supplemental Security Income (SSI) checks are called "gold checks" by the millions of senior citizens who receive them. The SSI is a federal check for certain low-income retired persons. (The amount of the check varies from state to state. In California, for example, a single person could get a total of $296 a month, a couple $552.) At present, the general qualifications for SSI are that you do not have cash or any other cashable assets of more than $1,500. You may own a home of any value, but if you own a car its value must not exceed $1,200.

It is important to note that you can work around the eligibility restrictions limiting your assets to $1,500. If you have more than $1,500 in cash, you could invest the money down to $1,499, which is just below the allowable limit. Or you could pay in advance for your burial needs, have your car overhauled, buy necessary clothing, have dental work done, fix up the house, or even give money to relatives—but not all in one week. Spread the purchases out over a six-month period.

Similarly, if your car is worth more than the allowable $1,200, you may still qualify for SSI if you use the car to go to the doctor, the pharmacy, or to other places for your health's sake. If you fit the requirements, don't tell the interviewer when you apply that you use your $3,000 car to go to the beach occasionally. That statement *may* disqualify you.

I have worked with hundreds of senior citizens in my home town who thought they were not eligible, but later discovered that they were. You don't need to receive a regular Social Security check to qualify, either. The benefits are worth investigating. So if you think you might be eligible, contact your local welfare office or Social Security office for full information.

PENSIONS

If your employer does not have a pension plan—start your own.

Anyone can have a pension plan. If you don't have one, you'd better start one if you want a decent retirement. If you are not covered by a company pension plan or any other plan, you can begin your own through what is called an Individual Retirement Account (IRA). IRA is a long-overdue plan now allowed by federal legislation enacted in 1974. An IRA permits you to set aside, tax free, up to 15 percent of your gross annual income, or a maximum of $1,500 a year. If you are self-employed, you are also entitled to start your own pension under the Keogh Plan, contributing up to 15 percent of your income, or a maximum of $7,500 tax free per year.

To help you understand the differences between the traditional company pensions, the Individual Retirement Account, and the Keogh Plan, let's take a look at all three.

Company Pensions

A good pension can make the difference between a retirement in which you have to scrimp to get by and one in which you are fairly comfortable. To get the pension you want, start monitoring things now, to make sure your plan is adequate and sufficient for your needs.

The pension reform law of 1974 accomplished two major things for private pension plans: (1) It provided strict guidelines for *vesting*, which is the procedure by which an employee becomes entitled to the retirement benefits contributed by the company to his pension. (2) It required that pension funds be *insured* to prevent employees from losing benefits in case their company went bankrupt.

Vesting

As an employee you are entitled to any contributions you have made to a pension plan when you leave the company. But, as explained earlier, you are not entitled to the contributions your employer makes to the plan until you have a vested interest in the plan. This was difficult in the past because employers required long years of service and a certain required age before the employee could retire. Federal legislation now restricts employers to one of these three alternatives for vesting their employees:

1. Twenty-five percent vesting at the end of five years, 5 percent for each of the following five years, 10 percent in each of the next five years, so that the employee is fully vested after fifteen years.
2. Full vesting after ten years of service.
3. Fifty percent vesting when an employee's age plus his or her years of service total forty-five. This increases 10 percent each succeeding year, until full vesting is reached. This is known as the Rule of 45, which also stipulates that an employee with ten years of service must be 50 percent vested even if age and years of service do not equal forty-five.

Pension Fund Insurance

In the past employees lost all or most pension benefits if either the company or the pension fund went broke. The 1974 reform law requires pension funds to maintain certain minimum funding standards. It also requires that the funds be insured with the Pension Benefit Guaranty Corporation of the Department of Labor. The Guaranty Corporation was set up by this law and was empowered to borrow up to $100 million from the federal treasury to begin operations. If a pension fund goes bankrupt or is otherwise terminated, the Guaranty Corporation guarantees employees vested benefits up to $750 a month.

This is all well and good and of great value, but there are still many unprotected areas of private company pension plans, such as lack of survivors' benefits or an automatic cost-of-living formula. Most private pension plans are also not "portable," which means that employees cannot transfer pension credits from one employer to another. (By contrast, the workability of portable pension plans has been proved in Europe, where they are fairly common.)

Finally, to be sure you receive your pension find out what the correct procedure is to receive your pension in your company. Some necessitate written application within a short period of time after retirement.

Pension payments vary widely from company to company. They may be as little as 10 percent of your final working salary or as high as 75 percent, although the latter is rare. Generally, blue-collar workers get a fixed sum when they retire, while white-collar workers receive a percentage amounting to about 1.5 percent of their final annual salary, multiplied by the number of years worked. On the average, pensions range from $1,500 annually for twenty years' service to under $2,000 for thirty years' service. I know a woman who worked for a major newspaper for seventeen years and retired with a pension of $66 a month. Unfortunately, her case is not all that rare.

How to Investigate Your Pension

The 1974 reform law requires "employers to provide each employee covered by the pension plan with a summary description of the plan and any modifications of the plan in a manner that readily could be understood by the average participant." So you can find out what you need to know about your private pension plan from your own company by contacting the personnel department and asking for the company's pension booklet. If you are a union member, go to the appropriate local union official. He probably knows more about the pension plan than the president of your company.

Former employees who have retired from your office within the past few years are another good source of information. You can often find them through a company club for retirees. Ask them how they are managing and if they are able to live on the amount received. If the pension plan your company offers is no good, they are in the best position to know.

When you investigate your company pension, there are ten questions you should get answered. I have listed the questions in the box below so that you can easily refer back to them.

HOW TO INVESTIGATE YOUR PENSION

1. Does the plan have survivors' benefits?
2. Does the plan include a cost-of-living increase?
3. Is the plan portable?
4. Which of the three federal vesting schedules is the company using?
5. How is your pension benefit computed? What percentage of your final working salary can you expect to get?
6. Does the plan require that you work a minimum number of hours per week, or months per year, to qualify?
7. Will your pension be cut if you take early retirement? How much? If it can be cut, does your company have a history of strongly encouraging early retirement among its employees?
8. Does the plan allow you to make extra contributions so you will be entitled to a larger pension?
9. Once you retire, are there any stipulations you should know about to prevent your company from canceling your pension, such as working for a competitor?
10. Is the average benefit currently paid out by the plan comparable to the benefit you have been told to expect when you retire?

When you ask your questions, don't be satisfied with "I think so" or evasive answers. Find out the facts. Remember you're not toying with a few dollars. Without your pension you may have to rely solely on Social Security, which just isn't enough.

Should You Change Jobs?

If you discover that your company pension plan provides an inadequate retirement income, I suggest you investigate the prospects of changing to a company with a better pension plan. Yes, I know changing jobs after a number of years is a bold move, but I did it, and it secured my future.

Be careful, though. Before you make a move, weigh how much time you have spent toward gaining a vested interest in your pension at your present company against how much time it will take you to get a vested interest at the new outfit. Perhaps you can use your talent and experience as bargaining power in exchange for special allowances regarding vesting in the new company's pension plan.

If you have already gained a vested interest but decide the plan is poor enough to warrant a job change, the 1974 reform law has made that kind of move easier for you. The new law allows employees leaving a job to take their vested pension benefits and deposit them in an Individual Retirement Account, one of the two new plans created to give pension benefits to persons not covered by company plans.

INDIVIDUAL RETIREMENT ACCOUNT AND KEOGH PLAN

Two good pension plans and tax shelters.

The Individual Retirement Account (IRA) and Keogh Plan are major breakthroughs for the person planning for a secure retirement. There are two major differences between the two plans: (1) You can put only $1,500 into the IRA, but $7,500 into the Keogh. (2) The Keogh Plan is designed for the self-employed.

Both plans have a lot going for them. They are good pension plans and excellent tax shelters. You pay no income taxes on the money you put into either plan since the money is deducted from your gross income before your taxes are computed. In effect, you are allowed to contribute—tax free—up to $1,500 or $7,500 a year and save what you would have paid in taxes to Uncle Sam and the state. That's a substantial tax break.

The money in your IRA or Keogh Plan is then allowed to accumulate tax free, even if it includes income earned by the plan, such as from mutual-fund dividends or interest. You don't pay taxes on any of the money until it is disbursed to you in retirement, but by then you will be in a much lower tax category.

The money you put into the IRA or Keogh Plan must remain in the account until you reach age fifty-nine and a half. Early withdrawal, except in the case of disability or death, subjects the money to penalty, generally a 10 percent additional income tax. If both you and your spouse are working, it is advisable for you to set up separate accounts. If only one is working, the working partner can contribute up to $1,750 a year to a joint husband-and-wife IRA, or can establish an IRA for each and contribute up to $875 a year in each. The accounts can be set up at your local bank, savings institution, insurance company, or with your stockbroker.

The money you earmark for your plan can be invested in a variety of secure ways, including high interest (7 to 8 percent) certificates of deposit at your bank, insurance policies, annuities, stocks, bonds, and mutual funds.

When considering your IRA or Keogh Plan, the type of investment plan to use is likely to be your most difficult decision. For example, you will be faced with such alternatives as these: If you set up your plan in a savings institution and die before you receive the full amount accrued in the plan, the remainder must be distributed to your spouse or designated heir. If you use certain available plans through an insurance company, you continue to receive the benefits until you die, even if your investment is exhausted, but if you die before your investment runs out the insurance company keeps the remaining money you have invested.

As with any other investment plan, you should be cautious when starting either plan. Because they are relatively new and becoming increasingly popular, many financial institutions are attempting to tap this large, new market. Some have launched massive sales campaigns and disseminated misleading and deceptive information.

So look carefully at any sales pitch to see what selling costs (mainly sales commissions) are included in the plan. They range from 0 to 50 percent of the amount you contribute during the first few years of the plan's life. Paying a high selling fee could cost you several thousand dollars.

Most savings institutions charge you nothing to set up either plan, except for a $5 to $10 custodial fee. Mutual fund dealers charge 1.5 to 9 percent, depending on whether or not a sales commission is involved, insurance companies an even higher amount.

How Much Should You Put into an IRA or Keogh Plan?

The amount of money you put into your IRA or Keogh Plan is crucial to making the plan work for you. As I stated, my advice is to put 15 percent of your gross income or the maximum allowable into the plan each year. If this is not possible, begin with an amount you can afford and as your income increases, increase the amount of your contribution as well. Most pension experts expect the government to raise the maximum amounts you can contribute to both plans periodically. The worst mistake you can make is to limit your contributions to a certain fixed amount every year without raising that amount as your income increases. Here's why.

If you were to save $1,500 a year for twenty years at an annual interest rate of 8 percent (which is roughly what you earn on a savings bank IRA plan), you will end up with about $75,000 at the end of the twenty years. Sounds good—but, again, it's misleading because it does not account for the effects of the estimated 5 percent annual inflation for those twenty years. When you consider that factor, the $75,000 you save will have a purchasing power in twenty years of only about $28,000 at today's inflationary rates. The reason it will drop in purchasing power so drastically is because each succeeding $1,500 you invest will have a decreased value compared to that in the previous year. The effect of putting away the same amount of money each year in the face of inflation is roughly equivalent to putting away a smaller amount of money each year. The only way to make sure your IRA or Keogh grows enough to offset inflation is to increase the amounts you contribute each year. Right now the maximum you can contribute is $1,500 even if you can afford more. However, most experts feel the government will raise the ceiling to keep up with rising incomes.

If you always contribute 15 percent, you can figure your earned income will increase at roughly the same rate as inflation. So each succeeding year you will be adding an increased, but adequate, amount of pension money.

The insidious effects of inflation are so serious that I can't help but refer to them frequently as I talk about your financial planning. Inflation is a thief, and unless you plan with its effects in mind, you are liable to end up with retirement income slashed by as much as two-thirds or more.

One more caution. The fact that the IRA and Keogh plans are government authorized does not mean that they are government insured or government regulated. As with insurance and investments there are good deals and bad deals, and you should thoroughly investigate your alternatives and give careful consideration to the company in which you are placing your trust.

Restrictions on Participation in an IRA

There are some restrictions to participation in an IRA. The main criterion is that you cannot set up your own IRA if you are a participant in any other pension plan. *You can be a participant of only one pension plan at a time.*

You are eligible to set up an IRA account only if:

1. You are not a participant in a company pension, bonus, or other stock-holding plan.
2. You are not a participant in an employer annuity or bond purchase plan.
3. You are not a participant in a retirement plan established by the government, such as a civil service retirement plan or a military retirement plan.
4. You are not a participant in an annuity program purchased by certain tax-exempt organizations, such as public schools.
5. You are not a participant in another self-employed pension plan, for example, the Keogh Plan.

You are eligible to contribute to an IRA plan, however, even if you are already receiving benefits from another retirement plan or are receiving Social Security.

IRA as an Alternative or a Supplement

If you have the option but do not participate in any of the five pension plans mentioned above, of if you find your company pension inadequate, you may find it more beneficial to forego the company plan and establish the IRA.

If your employer has a pension plan which will take a few years before you are eligible to join, but which you must join, you can begin an IRA plan in the meantime.

If, as mentioned earlier, you lose or quit your job after building up vested benefits, you may take all the money you have coming and place it into your own IRA, with no limit on the amount you put in. (It is important to keep in mind, however, that you have only sixty days from the time you receive the money to make the transfer to IRA.) And you don't have to pay taxes on that money. For example, if you lose or quit your job after you contribute to a company pension plan for ten years, you probably have accumulated several thousand dollars that you may take out and deposit immediately into an IRA without paying taxes on that sum. If such a situation arises, transferring your accumulated money to IRA is a sound alternative to spending the money and on which you are required to pay taxes.

Later, if you work for a company that does have a pension plan, the law allows you to take your entire IRA contribution and invest it in the company pension plan, provided the new employer consents. If the employer consents, you cannot contribute to IRA if you join the company plan. If the employer does not consent, you may continue to maintain and contribute to the IRA.

To repeat, you can contribute to only one retirement plan at a time. This does not, however, preclude your investing in other areas.

Restrictions on Participation in a Keogh Plan

The Keogh Plan is open to the following:

1. Self-employed people. This includes any person who pays a self-employment tax under the federal Social

Security system or any person who elects to come under that system by paying the self-employment tax. This category also includes any person who owns less than 10 percent of a partnership.

2. Owner-employees of a business. This includes any self-employed individual who is a sole owner or who has a partnership greater than 10 percent of the business. A partnership plan is set up in the name of the partnership by whomever has controlling interest (that is, more than 50 percent in the company). This may include one or more partners. A partner with less than controlling interest may set up a plan with the consent of the other partners, even though the others may not choose to participate.

3. Employees of the self-employed, also known as common-law employees. These are people who own no part of the business but who work for a self-employed person or a partnership.

You don't have to be a full-time employee to qualify for the Keogh Plan. If you hold a regular job and are covered by a corporate or government pension there, you can start a Keogh Plan on earnings from part-time work. To illustrate, if you work for Chrysler Corporation as a mechanic or manager and operate your own garage on a part-time basis, the money you earn from the garage (which is your own business) may be used to start a Keogh Plan.

An information booklet on Individual Retirement Accounts and Keogh Plans is available free at Internal Revenue Service district offices or from the Pension Benefit Guaranty Corporation, 2020 K Street, N.W., Washington, D.C. 20006. The IRS also has a free booklet explaining the plans: Publication 590, "Tax Information on Individual Retirement Savings Programs." However, if you are dealing with a large amount of money, it is best to consult an accountant.

OTHER INVESTMENT ALTERNATIVES

The best investment you can make is to own your own home.

It is not the purpose of this book to give specific investment advice nor to detail the investment alternatives that you should be considering. I will be satisfied that I have done my job in this area if you accept the absolute necessity of hard and careful thinking about your financial future, and if you are prepared to start thinking about it now.

When you begin to study investment alternatives, I highly recommend you sit down with a copy of *Funk & Wagnalls Guide to Personal Money Management* by C. Colburn Hardy. It explains the possibilities in plain language and gives sound advice on the relative merits and liabilities of each situation. The one investment I can urge you to make without hesitation is the time, effort, and few dollars involved in buying and reading that book.

The experts rank various forms of savings and investments in different orders of desirability, based on their areas of expertise, personal experience, their clients' needs, and the statistics on which they are basing their calculations. But you must examine whatever you read in the light of your own experience.

For many readers, stocks and bonds bought individually or through mutual funds will be the most desirable balance of risk and growth. Indeed, investing in high-quality stocks over a long period has proved to be a sound method of placing money. Between 1926 and 1965—including the disastrous years of the Great Depression—the average stock on the New York Stock Exchange yielded a return in growth and dividends of 9.3 percent.

Another investment you might look into is real estate, which is generally considered to have the highest degree of risk and the potential for the highest annual percentage of return. Annuities, savings accounts, insurance, and other forms of investments are possibilities that should all be considered. The choice depends not only on the amount being invested but also on the psychology of the investor—especially his or her ability to accept risks.

Let me briefly give you the benefit of my experience in this area. I have frequently reminded you about the assault of inflation on the retired person's plans. Time after time I have seen the harshest effects of inflation strike those people who put all of their savings into insurance company annuities and savings accounts.

Annuities are contracts between an individual and a life insurance company, in which the life insurance company agrees to pay a specific amount of money to the annuity purchaser after that purchaser has reached a certain age. Although it does offer a guaranteed income (but for the possibility of corporate failure) and there is no risk, that income is generally fixed and totally subject to the eroding effects of inflation.

For much the same reason I dislike ordinary passbook savings accounts, the most popular type of savings account, which currently have an interest rate of 5¼ percent. Since inflation in our time seems to be set at a considerably higher percentage, the interest from one's savings is completely wiped out by a 5½ percent inflation rate. Even if the rate of inflation is only 5¼ percent your savings would not be keeping pace, for interest on savings is income and is taxed accordingly. For example, if you have $10,000 in a regular passbook account earning 5¼ percent annual interest, you would have $525 in interest at the end of the year. If you are in the 25 percent tax bracket you would pay some $131 in taxes on the interest, bringing your after-tax interest down to less than 4 percent.

Where should you invest your money? My general recommendation is that one of the soundest investments you can make for your own retirement is to own your own home. If you don't own one now, I recommend that you buy one. To begin with, you can live in it now; it offers many tax advantages over the years on mortgage payments; and in addition, it will probably appreciate in value. If you already own a house, you might consider buying another one and renting it out. If the rent does nothing more than pay for the mortgage, upkeep, and taxes while your property appreciates, you will have made a good investment. If possible, purchase the second house near water or in the mountains and use it as a vacation retreat or rent it out during holidays at the higher rental rates such properties attract.

With good planning you will own two houses free and clear by the time you retire. At that time the rent on one may pay the tax bills for both and provide extra income. If you choose to sell one after you retire, you can convert the cash into another form of retirement investment, when the decision about what kind of retirement income you will need will be much clearer.

Above all, my advice is never to sell your house to live in an apartment. That's one mistake retired people make that is hard to undo. Once you sell, inflation may outrun your ability to buy another house and you may find that your rent is constantly pushing against your ability to pay. The only reason you should ever consider selling your house is to buy another one better suited to your needs.

Life insurance (what kind, how much, from whom), like other investment alternatives, is an extraordinarily complex and highly individual matter. In addition to being a form of protection, life insurance can also be a form of investment—and certainly should be one element that is taken into consideration by anyone planning his or her financial future. For helpful information on insurance, I recommend two books: *Your Insurance Handbook* by Richard Guarino and Richard Trubo, and *What's Wrong with Your Life Insurance* by Norman F. Dacey.

HIDDEN FINANCIAL ASSETS OF
THE RETIRED

Discovering them is your responsibility.

Many retired people do not know about a wide variety of
financial breaks that are available to them. Some of these
are granted by the federal government and derived from our
ever-changing income tax laws. At present, some retired
people need not file a federal income tax return. These are
single people sixty-five and over, with an income less than
$3,100; couples with income less than $4,900 (including
Social Security).

People over sixty-five are also entitled to extra exemp-
tions and such benefits as a tax-free allowance on the sale of
their home. Retirement income credits are available for
those who get little in the way of tax-free Social Security.
In order to find out about all of these benefits, one must
stay abreast of federal income tax laws. A booklet called
"Your Federal Income Tax" is available free from the
Internal Revenue Service. The standard income tax books
that appear every year in the bookstores also contain information in these areas. Further facts may be obtained from
Tax Facts, c/o NRTA-AARP, 1909 K Street, N.W., Washington, D.C. 20049.

Your local senior center or Social Security office may
well be able to tell you about tax breaks in your own
community which may not be permitted elsewhere. In California, for example, a variety of property tax breaks are
available, as is a renter's refund. But they won't do the
California senior citizen any good if he or she doesn't find
out about them. And, as with all the other tax breaks,
loopholes, and special tax-saving opportunitites, the knowledge of them is often hard-won and comes only through a
vigorous pursuit of the facts. But it is there for those with
the perseverance to track it down.

RING YOUR SPOUSE

Ignorance isn't bliss.

Securing your future through the acquisition of all that you are entitled to under Social Security and pensions, besides all that you can milk from your savings and investments, is not the full battle. Securing those hard-won victories for your spouse is also an important part of eliminating the retirement threat.

If you are married, begin thinking about the type of life your surviving spouse may have in the event of your death. Although death is not a pleasant topic to think about, it is a necessary one if you are to insure your spouse's security after you are gone. Plans should be made now in the event you die before your spouse does. This should not be an unpleasant emotional experience. It should be just one more financial consideration that figures into your retirement planning. Once careful plans have been made, you can take great comfort in the fact that your survivor will be as safe and secure as possible.

But don't leave your spouse in the dark when it comes to the financial planning you have made. This can easily happen because in most families either the husband or wife keeps track of the finances, pays the bills, handles the checking and savings accounts, and so on. This can be a deplorable matter if the death of one leaves the other in total ignorance, with no mate to call on to answer vital questions.

As retirement approaches, begin to educate your spouse in as many financial matters as you can. Insist that he or she pay the bills with you, learn how to handle the bank accounts, and pay the insurance premiums. If you are the one in the dark, insist that your mate teach you all the financial aspects of your life. Both husband and wife should handle these together. When a decision is made to buy or sell anything, such as a car or stocks, talk the details over together. If a change in an insurance policy is contemplated, the two of you should examine the documents and talk to the insurance agent. Don't let only one of you be the financial expert. Both of you should be.

I know that many men feel their wives are not capable of handling financial matters. That's foolish thinking. If you think she is not capable now, do you suppose she will suddenly become more capable after you are dead and gone? I've known a lot of overwrought widows who don't even know how to make their next house payment or insurance premiums, let alone keep up with stocks, bonds, or other assets their husbands left them.

To make the transition easier, make sure your spouse knows where all important documents are kept. Prepare a list of them and attach it to your other important papers. The list should include all assets (both separate and joint) and a note as to where they are located, all information pertaining to stock certificates (including the names and addresses of any brokers involved), all insurance documents, and a copy of your will.

WILLS

Estate planning is a must.

A lot of smart people don't have wills. They are a lot less smart than they think they are. Having a will is the only way to be sure that your assets are distributed in accordance with your wishes. In a will you declare your intentions regarding your assets and name an executor (male) or executrix (female) to carry out those wishes. If you leave no will, a court will appoint an administrator to dispose of the estate in accordance with state laws. State laws may take heavy tax bites from your assets, and those whom you wanted to provide for may not inherit as much as you intended.

Your spouse may also suffer hardship because upon the death of one party many states automatically freeze bank accounts and safety deposit boxes until tax liability is determined. Your spouse may have to survive on whatever cash he or she has on hand until the state acts. This might be weeks or even months if there are unforeseen complications.

State laws are not always kind to the remaining spouse when it comes to division of property among several heirs. Some states allow a spouse 50 percent of the assets; others 33 percent. Even more devastating is the possibility that without a will your spouse could end up living in a home owned by a relative both of you dislike.

Although some states allow you to prepare your own will, called a holographic will, a trip to an estate planning lawyer is the wisest procedure to take. It's a one-time expense, unless you decide to modify or change your will later.

If you are an extremely efficient person, however, and take care to examine available state literature on how to prepare your own will, the holographic will may serve your purposes very well. Still, homemade wills are sometimes contested by greedy relatives.

Choose the executor of your will with care, for he or she acts in your stead when you die. The executor chooses the probate attorney; inventories your assets; pays federal, state, and inheritance taxes; obtains a decree of distribution from the court; and changes ownership of the assets to your heirs. It is not a job to give to your Aunt Agatha. It is a job for a trusted, competent person, preferably one known to your heirs. You may want to name co-executors, such as a family member and your attorney. The trust department of your bank, which has experts in such matters, also may act as the executor.

Probate is the processing of your will through the probate court to establish its validity and legality. The process is guided by your will's executor, although he or she will appoint an attorney—probably your estate planning lawyer—to act as the legal representative. The person you appoint as executor is completely in charge of carrying out your wishes, as expressed in your will.

Since the first job of the executor is to inventory your assets, you can plan ahead and do the executor and your heirs a big favor by leaving an inventory of your major assets in a designated place with a copy of your will.

If a delay does occur in probating the will (for example, if someone contests the will), your spouse will need some money on which to live. This can be accomplished by naming your wife as the beneficiary of your life insurance policy since this money does not need to go through the court. It is paid directly to your beneficiary with little delay.

Estate taxes can take sizable chunks out of your estate. The rules here changed in 1977. Under the old rule if your estate was worth $60,000 (this included such things as a car, house, savings account), you had to pay taxes on that portion of your estate worth more than $60,000. Under the new law the minimum is now $120,000, and by 1981 the figure will be over $175,000. In addition, the new law allows one to leave a spouse either half of the estate or $250,000—whichever is larger—tax-free. If your financial assets are worth more, your lawyer can help you find ways to reduce taxes when you are planning your will. One of the ways that people used to avoid certain estate taxes was to give away assets prior to their death because gift taxes were lower than estate taxes. Now, however, they are the same. The permutations and combinations of estate planning are as varied as the ingenuity of your estate planning attorney, whose knowledge of these laws you should call upon.

YOUR ULTIMATE SECURITY

Four steps you must take.

We've discussed many ways to help secure your financial retirement in this chapter. You can see it's not the easiest thing in the world to accomplish. And if you are in your mid-fifties or over, this is even more difficult because you will not be able to amass the large amount of dollars needed to maintain your present standard of living in retirement. That means you will have to supplement your retirement funds by continuing to work. That is not as bad as it may seem, despite what some younger readers may think.

If you're in your forties and fifties, maybe you can hardly wait for the day when you retire. But people in their late fifties and early sixties feel just the opposite. They dread that day because they feel they will be stepping out of the mainstream of everyday American life. You need dread no more. The next chapter will help prepare you for new and exciting retirement careers.

Other steps can be taken without putting money aside or planning to work. You can plan to be healthy (Chapter 7), you can plan to fight to achieve helpful legislation (Chapter 8), and you can begin innovative programs to give retirees continuing responsibilities and deserved rights and freedoms (Chapters 9 and 10).

You may not be able to cure the disease of retirement, but you may be able to prevent it if you start now.

6 PLAN TO WORK: Preparing for Your Second Career

Stepping out of the labor force is like stepping on a land mine.

If you aren't already among those fortunate enough to have some skill or knowledge in a field with which you can earn an income in retirement, I firmly advise you to develop one. For most people, this ability to continue working and earning money is a necessary supplement to pensions, savings, investments, and Social Security—besides the important consideration of being a source of involvement in daily life. If I can convince you of the wisdom of that advice, I will have accomplished one of the most important aspects of retirement planning.

Let me illustrate its significance by telling you about two retired men I know—both in their late sixties, both with pensions—whose lives have become very different from each other because of this very thing—only one of them planned to work after retirement.

Phil, an electronics engineer for an Eastern firm, was offered early retirement so his company could cut costs. They added the inducement of a slightly higher pension than was actually due him, further implying that there was a good chance that his job would be eliminated anyway. So Phil retired on about $500 a month—not a bad sum ten years ago—and took a few engineering jobs on the side to earn extra income.

At first, those special assignments were easy enough to come by, especially since he did not want too many. Now, ten years later. inflation has drastically reduced his pension, which had no cost-of-living escalator, and he is having trouble getting the odd jobs because of his age and because his contact with people handling employment is growing less and less. Moreover, he failed to keep abreast of the changes in his professional field. He has no other skills that he can fall back onto in order to get a decent paying job. As a result, this former professional's standard of living has been cut in half.

The other man, Bob, was a former Air Force pilot, then a commercial pilot for a small airline, before he developed a physical tremor that forced him to retire with a pension of $550 a month. But a few years before retiring, he did some thinking and some planning. He decided that he wanted to continue working, not only to occupy his time in a satisfying way but also to maintain his preretirement income. So while he was still fully employed, Bob used much of his spare time gaining experience at his hobby, which was photography. To learn more, he studied magazines and books from the library and took courses at night. In addition, he took a class in picture framing so he could properly display the results of his hobby.

When he retired, Bob used part of his savings to buy some basic photo lab equipment and rented a small store just off a shopping mall. Here he set up his own photo-enlarging and framing studio. Through an ad in the local newspaper, he located a retired carpenter to help him build a darkroom in the back of the store, then bought some used furniture that he repaired to make a comfortable waiting room in the front of the studio.

Bob advertised in the local newspaper as a photographer specializing in enlarging and framing family photographs. He now has a nice, small, low-overhead business which doesn't take all of his time.

I asked him what he would have done if the photo studio hadn't worked out, either because it was in the wrong location or because he just got tired of it. I love his answer. "Then I would have started something else. There are plenty of other things I can do." When I asked, "Like what?" he quickly responded, "Whatever interests me. I'm not going to let retirement get the best of me. I can always learn how to capitalize on the things I know how to do."

I wish I could teach everyone to have that attitude, because people like Bob will never have to worry about growing poor in retirement—or bored.

There are various reasons why retired people often find themselves cut off from the job market, so let me suggest some ways you can prepare yourself to continue to compete for jobs, even after retirement.

STAYING WITHIN THE RESTRICTIONS OF SOCIAL SECURITY

Making the law work for you.

A major obstacle you will have to contend with after you learn a marketable skill for retirement is the Social Security Administration. According to Social Security rules, if a retired person collecting Social Security earns more than $3,000 in a year, he or she loses benefits at the rate of $1 for every $2 of earnings over that amount during any month that the income exceeds $250. This earnings restriction is called the Social Security "retirement test" and is one of those not-too-talked-about rules that affect you when you retire. (Earnings that do not apply to the retirement test include income from pensions, stock dividends, annuities, rents, savings account interest, veterans' benefits, inheritances, gain from the sale of a capital asset, gifts, or royalties.)

In effect, the restriction affects the younger retiree who relies solely on Social Security and is discouraged from improving his financial situation by working. It does not apply in any way to retirees over the age of seventy-two. They can make as much as they are able, without penalty.

Many people now living within the current Social Security laws still manage to receive fairly substantial salary payments which would disqualify them for the receipt of much of their Social Security benefits. Instead they arrange to receive these large payments during only two months of the year, thereby taking advantage of the provision that you lose your Social Security payments only during the months in which the received income exceeds $250. (Remember you are entitled to your full monthly benefit if you earn less than $250 a month.)

Here are some ways you might live within this restriction, depending on your working status:

1. Under the present law, you can arrange for an understanding employer to pay you a very large salary one month, and a much smaller salary—just under the retirement test limit—all the other months in which you want to collect your Social Security benefits.
2. If you are self-employed, follow the same principle. Gear your operation for one big month of maximum earnings, so that when you sacrifice your Social Security benefit for that month it will be a worthwhile sacrifice. During the other months, pay yourself just under the retirement test limit. Be honest about when you earned the money.
3. If you are financially able, there is one more consideration: forego your entire Social Security benefit between sixty-five and seventy-two. What happens is that the Social Security benefit eventually received will

increase by 1 percent for each year between the ages of sixty-five and seventy-two that you declined to collect benefits. For many people, the feeling of being a useful member of society by continuing to work is worth the sacrifice of seven years of Social Security benefits.

Social Security rules are subject to change. In fact, Congress is now considering a bill that would allow Social Security to prorate your annual earnings over the entire year, thus eliminating the possibility of receiving a very large salary in one month and still receive benefits during the other months of the year, as mentioned in the first point above. But the maximum amount you are allowed to earn and still be eligible for your full Social Security benefit is likely to be raised in the near future to a new retirement test limit of $7,000. But if the law remains the same, it is never wise to break it or even bend it to your advantage. It is always appropriate to know the law so well that you can take advantage of any provision which allows you to make yourself comfortable while still following the law. Your job is to remain as wise about what the law allows you to do as the government is about what the law forbids you to do.

PREPARING FOR YOUR SECOND CAREER

A marketable skill is money in your pocket.

Of course, it may be difficult to feel the need for retirement planning if you're in your early forties since retirement seems a long way off. Nevertheless, you would be smart to begin planning.

But if you are in your fifties and your financial future seems pretty well determined, there is little time to waste. Now is the time to take the prospect of retirement seriously and start considering what other jobs may be within the scope of your interest and skill, for the ability to work is your greatest asset in retirement. If you have a marketable skill, you can always have money in your pocket.

Although positions in the usually-thought-of job market are limited, there are still many thousands of jobs available to the retired. The key to getting one of them is to prepare yourself by learning a marketable skill *before you retire.*

Some lowering of job expectations might be necessary. If your company retired you from a prestigious managerial position where you directed activities of a dozen employees, there is little chance you will find the exact same position in retirement. Accepting this will require separating your self-image from the kind of work you do. Remember that by the time you retire, you've already had one career that brought you a measure of status and success. The reason for your second career is to earn enough extra money to make your retirement comfortable and also to provide a sense of satisfaction, productivity, and self-worth.

My friend Tom is a good example of this. He is a highly paid senior engineer for a large company. Although only forty, he prepared for retirement early by learning locksmithing and typewriter repair by taking all the night school and correspondence courses he could. And he ended up becoming very expert at both trades. To find out what his newly acquired skills were worth, Tom advertised for business in the local newspaper. Within six months he had so much work that he spent evenings and weekends fixing typewriters and locks. His preparing this early is really paying off, for he was delighted to discover that he made almost as much money working part-time as he did at his full-time engineering job. Now whenever Tom decides to retire, he knows he has those money-making skills waiting to be put to use.

There are other people who already have an extremely marketable skill that can be easily adapted to a retirement profession. Accountants, bookkeepers, barbers, realtors, typists, tutors, lawyers, and doctors never have to retire until they are too ill to work. Other occupations—some self-employable—remain marketable no matter what your age may be: business consultants; auto, real estate, and insurance sales persons; motel or apartment managers; all types of appliance repairpersons, and a variety of jobs in the trades and professions.

LEARNING A NEW SKILL

All you need is the desire.

If you don't have a skill that can be adapted to retirement, you can acquire one with a three-month investment of time by taking night classes in a high school or local college. Most community and state colleges have free adult education programs with only a small registration fee required. Generally, the only qualification you need is a desire to learn. And learning a new skill is not as difficult as many adults believe. Learning does not diminish with age. Look at me. When I was sixty-seven I took several courses in night school. Within a year I was qualified in the basics of automotive, television, and refrigeration repair. You can do the same.

You can begin the process by listing all the skills you might like to learn. Select those that appear to have the highest marketability and those with the highest potential of being performed in your own home. Call up local high schools and community colleges. Talk to one of the educational counselors about your goals and find out if the school offers courses in those fields.

The opportunities are there if you want to take them, as evidenced by the fact that the largest growth of any section of the educational market is being experienced by the various adult education courses.

These are available in just one high school:

bookkeeping
data processing
medical secretarial procedures
medical or nursing assistant
office machines
income tax preparation
real estate principles
shorthand
small business management
interior decorating
sewing machine maintenance
tailoring and dress design
auto mechanics
blueprint reading
cabinet making
electronics
television repair

In addition, there are all kinds of homemaking, crafts, recreation, and general education courses offered at churches, retirement villages, recreation and community centers.

Some of the more highly technical skills may cost a few hundred dollars at a commercial school. But that's not a bad investment for a valuable piece of retirement security. You may even be able to deduct the cost of the course from your taxes.

You might also consider correspondence courses offered by the commercial schools. These are usually advertised in specialty magazines that pertain to the field in which you are interested.

Also bear in mind that you can acquire a new skill as a hobby now, with its becoming a source of retirement income later. Currently, there is a renaissance of the old-fashioned crafts, such as crocheting lap robes, decorating clothes with embroidery, macrameing plant hangers, picture framing, knitting sweaters and afghans, leatherwork, pottery, jewelry-making in silver and gold, old-fashioned cabinet work (spice racks, medicine chests), and furniture making. Even the art of creating stained glass windows has become extremely popular and profitable.

All these crafts are offered in night school classes, free or for a small fee. The items you make may be sold through distributors available through the local craft guild. Even if you never use these skills to supplement your retirement income, they can still be pleasurable hobbies and a great source of money-saving gifts.

If you do decide to learn a new profession, you might even take it a couple of steps further and learn two or three. It's as good as money in the bank.

MARKETABLE JOBS FOR RETIREES

Your objective is money, not prestige.

Below are a few examples of highly marketable job possibilities. They are listed in no particular order. Since both preretired and retired people's interests and circumstances are so diverse, I make no attempt to suggest which ones you should pursue. (William David's book, *Not Quite Ready to Retire,* and other books at your local library have more complete listings of job possibilities for retirees.)

Business Consultant

Business people need not throw away their briefcases merely because they retire. Thousands of new businesses come into existence each year. More than half of them fold, often because of poor management. The business skills acquired during your career make you uniquely qualified to advise these inexperienced entrepreneurs. And if you have thirty or forty years' experience you, no doubt, have enough valuable information at your fingertips to spell the difference between profit and loss for these new businesses.

Retirement is often viewed as a place from which a person cannot return to the business world. That's simply not true if you go about it in the right way. You may have trouble getting hired at sixty-five by major established companies who are afraid you'll boost their pension and worker's compensation costs, but that's not where you should apply for a job. Go to the young businesses that need your experience. Demonstrate some of what you know. You'd be surprised how many will listen to you, especially if they are sharp enough to have the success of their fledgling business foremost in their minds.

Prepare a resume and letter to emphasize the managerial skills that you can bring to their company. Mail them to the small businesses in your area you'd like to work for.

Community organizations, such as the Senior Corps of Retired Executives (SCORE) and the Small Business Administration (SBA), can also direct you to many new companies in your area.

Appliance Repair Service

The cost of having an electrician or appliance serviceperson come to your home is, as everyone knows, inordinately high. Since the average consumer has no idea how to fix household appliances, "authorized" repair companies can diagnose and charge whatever they wish. Thus an independent repairperson with little overhead and nobody to split the profits with can afford to give generous discounts. Clearly, such a qualified person would be welcomed into any household.

A night school course could qualify you to repair refrigerators, stoves, air conditioners, televisions, radios, most motor-driven kitchen appliances, lawnmowers, washing

machines and dryers, and most office equipment, such as
typewriters, dictaphones and tape recorders. The field is
open to any man or woman with a little mechanical apti-
tude and the motivation to learn.

Once you have qualified yourself in such a skill, you can
set yourself up in an independent business, advertise in the
classifieds and by word of mouth, charge less than authorized dealers, and still make a handsome retirement salary. If
you are still too young to put your retirement skill to work,
use it as a job on the side or practice on your own
appliances.

Starting such an independent business is as easy as you
want it to be. The potential market is there and crying for
competent servicepeople who are less expensive and give
faster service. All you need do is let those people know
where you are.

Bookkeeping and Tax Preparation

High schools and community colleges always offer free or
inexpensive evening courses in bookkeeping and tax preparation. Many businesses hire older workers as bookkeepers,
and smaller businesses often allow their bookkeeping to be
done as a part-time job in the home. Each year there are
about 75,000 openings for such bookkeepers, according to
one expert in retirement opportunities, so it's a good one to
consider.

Income tax preparation is a lucrative skill to have, but it
is seasonal. If you are qualified, you can work hard seven
days a week from January 1 to April 15 of each year, and
then take the rest of the year off. It's an occupation that
either a woman or a man can use prior to retirement to
supplement income.

It works very well for one retired man I know who
supports himself, his wife, and his big old house by preparing people's taxes in his own home. He charges between

$15 and $50, depending on the complexity of the job. He is highly sought-after because he stays abreast of his field by studying new tax laws.

Auto Mechanics

Most night schools offer courses in basic auto repair, for which you'll have to go to school a bit longer unless you are particularly mechanically inclined. Auto mechanics need never retire, even if they have been retired. More than one mechanic retired from a large repair shop has outfitted his van with all the tools he needed. From his "Garage on Wheels" he can perform all the auto repair services anyone might need, right in his own driveway. He can reach potential customers through advertisements in flyers and classified sections of local newspapers. Because he doesn't have the overhead of maintaining a garage, he is able to charge much less than the average gas station and still make a good profit. The result can be that his take-home pay is higher than it was before he retired.

Sales

Even if you have never sold anything before, you could create a successful retirement career as a salesperson. Small retail operations often have trouble keeping part-time employees working at minimum wages. Mature retired people seem made-to-order for this situation.

You might also consider attending night school in order to obtain a realtor's license to sell real estate. You must pass a state exam to get your license, but a night school course will equip you to pass the test. You're certainly never too old to learn a new profession, and real estate can be a highly lucrative field and not that difficult to crack if you have drive.

Day Care for Children

Most parents prefer a mature babysitter for their children rather than a teenager, and although the pay isn't always fantastic, the rewards and pleasures are. One of your rewards from this kind of work is an intimate association with a child eager to learn from someone who has had more experiences than children can imagine.

If you like to teach children and organize games, you should offer your services to a day-care center. The job opportunities are numerous, particularly for men, since there are so few in the field and because men seldom think of themselves in that role and consequently seldom opt for it.

Tutoring

If you have a thorough knowledge of any subject—photography, dressmaking, carpentry, public speaking, foreign languages, piano, or typing—why not get paid to teach it? You can advertise through your local newspaper and on school and market bulletin boards.

There are hundreds of other examples. I've just given you a few to show what is available to the retiree or to the smart pre-retiree who understands the importance of preparing for the future now. I hope you're convinced that you need to be self-reliant, for it is your own ability, your own talents and interests that will make your retirement life comfortable. You know what your talents and interests are. If you don't have *anything* on tap now, develop *something* to achieve your goal of a secure and happy retirement.

SOME POINTERS ON GETTING A
JOB AFTER SIXTY-FIVE

It's easier than you think.

Getting a job after age sixty-five is easier than you think, but it depends largely on your perseverance and drive. It took me six months of harassing the county and state government to convince them to hire me as a senior citizens coordinator. At first, they told me I was too old (I was sixty-nine), but they finally hired me after much persistence on my part when I showed them what I could do. Now in my seventies, I'm still on the job. My second career required little more than adapting my talent for business organization to organizing senior programs. And it worked well.

Above all, don't let your age inhibit you when you look for a job. The young often tend to look upon seniors as the used-up portion of the working population. They think age makes less efficient workers than youth.

They are dead wrong. Every reliable survey has shown that older employees are more dedicated, more dependable, more conscientious, and have less absenteeism than younger employees. They require less supervision, take their jobs more seriously, and have a greater sense of responsibility and loyalty to their employers. Their experience, more acute judgment, and maturity make them more efficient. They get along better with fellow workers. They are capable of greater concentration because they are distracted by fewer outside matters such as domestic and personal problems. They have come to terms with themselves.

These are your assets and you would do well to let a prospective employer who seems reticent to hire you know about them.

It helps to be confident about yourself. If you apply for a job with a defeatist attitude, you probably will be defeated. The confidence you have in your own ability is often readily detected in your manner and speech. Employers are reluctant to hire someone who doesn't believe in himself or herself—no matter what age—because chances are that attitude translates itself into poor performance on the job. Employers want energetic, enthusiastic employees, because those are the ones most likely to do good work.

When you apply for a job, keep in mind that you are trying to sell yourself. This could be the most crucial factor in your landing the job. So show your potential employer the vitality and desire you have to work.

Plenty of the jobs go begging because too many sixty-five-year olds are convinced that nobody wants to hire them—so they don't try. If you want a job, you can get one, but you must be *persistent.* If you don't get a job after your first, second, or third interview, don't give up. Reassess your approach and try again.

WHERE TO LOOK

Jobs are everywhere—if you know where to look.

Once you're ready to look, make your first stop the State Employment Services Office. For the one in your area, look in the telephone book under your state government listings. Many of the more than 2,000 local offices across the country have "older-worker counselors" and retraining services available and are happy to give job counseling and placement assistance. They can also direct you to local nonprofit employment agencies that cater to the needs of older workers. Some of these, such as Manpower and Olsten's, specialize in placing older workers in temporary positions. Other agencies in your area are listed in the telephone directory under such names as Senior Citizens Employment, Mature Personnel, Senior Personnel Placement, and so forth. Free job counseling services can also be found at many branches of the "Y" and Salvation Army.

If you are a man or woman with a professional or executive background, look into the telephone directory for the nearest Forty-Plus Club. This organization specializes in finding jobs for senior executives and professionals. Members must spend twenty hours a week operating the club by locating job prospects and helping others find jobs. When a member finds a job, he or she resigns the membership. The club has a good record. Their contacts in the business world are extensive and their placement rate high.

Mature Temps, Inc., another excellent job placement service for older workers, is sponsored by the National Retired Teachers Association (NRTA) and the American Association of Retired Persons (AARP). The jobs are usually temporary.

Retired military personnel can seek counseling and job placement services from the Department of Defense Referral Program, Transitional Manpower Programs, Office of the Assistant Secretary of Defense, Washington, D.C. 20201.

Senior Centers generally have job placement services for older workers. If the one near you doesn't, they might be able to direct you to places that do.

Clubs and associations, such as the Kiwanis and Masons, are good sources for job information. If you belong to such groups, send the word out among fellow members that you are looking for a job.

(For additional information, refer to Appendixes A and B at the end of this book.)

Don't overlook friends. Let them know you're looking for work. The grapevine often carries tips no organization ever hears about. Most good jobs, in fact, get filled through just such personal contacts and recommendations.

But, once again, the most important piece of advice I can give you is simply this: plan to work. Not only does your financial security depend on it, but so do your health and happiness.

Margaret Mead, the noted anthropologist, said it best on her seventy-fifth birthday. When asked about her future plans, she explained she was busy writing a new book, was planning a trip to Bali, and continuing work on several research projects. Her interview ended with these memorable words: "I fully intend to die, but I have no plans to retire."

7 PLAN TO BE HEALTHY: Staying Active in Body and Mind

What you do for yourself in your forties and fifties will pay dividends for the rest of your life.

I am about to tell you what you already know, and what I hope you will do is convert your knowledge into action. The advice may seem self-evident, and therefore unnecessary, but most of the retired people I know who knew these things when they were younger, and didn't do anything about them, are in rough shape today.

Nothing can ruin all your retirement planning quicker than poor health, especially poor health that burdens you with huge medical bills. Since many of the physical miseries of old age are the result of neglect, they can be prevented if you start early enough to take better care of your body. So, just as you should start securing your future finances while you're still young, you should also start ensuring your future physical and mental health. Let's look at how you can stay healthy and how you can avoid heavy medical bills with intelligent health insurance and planning.

BE HEALTHY, STAY HEALTHY

Today's habits, tomorrow's illness.

Many people take better care of their cars than they do of their bodies. But maintaining physical and mental health is like maintaining an automobile, and abuse and neglect will subtract years from your life just as it will from your car. If you wait until you retire, it may be too late. Certainly, it is easier to decide to be healthy before you are sixty-five than afterward. Although it is usually fruitless to advise people to do something today so they can enjoy the benefits in twenty years, I can only tell you that those retired people who took the time to acquire the habits of health invariably feel that it was the wisest investment of their lives.

For people over forty-five the leading causes of illness and death are heart disease, cancer, stroke, accidents, and cirrhosis of the liver. Your chances of getting heart disease are a lot less if you watch your eating and other physical habits. Too many fatty foods, excess weight, smoking, and lack of exercise will not help. The chances, or at least the effects, of cancer can be minimized with frequent checkups since many types are curable if detected in time. Certainly stopping smoking will drastically reduce your chances of getting lung cancer, mouth and throat cancer, and emphysema.

Drinking also needs to be controlled. A lot of deaths directly or indirectly caused by drinking are blamed on other things: accidents, coronary problems, "natural causes." If you find you like to drink a lot now—and if anyone hints you may be drinking too much—talk to someone or some organization about it. I'm not against drinking, but we live in a society where you almost don't have the right to say no to a drink. Drinking causes a lot of problems, and going into retirement sick may be worse than not getting there at all.

Be Physically Active

The way to longevity is exercise. That's what the doctors and physiologists say. Exercising prevents physical and mental abilities from deteriorating as fast.

On average, those who exercise regularly live longer than those who don't. Certainly they will stay healthier longer. Exercise makes the blood circulate better, keeps heart and lungs strong, improves the digestion, and of course keeps limbs active. I know I'm not saying anything new, but maybe if I say it enough there'll be some people who don't need to hear it several years from now.

People who are completely sedentary are four or five times more likely to die sooner than those who exercise consistently. With exercise there is less risk of heart attacks and strokes, and recovery from heart ailments is more rapid.

The benefits of exercise are more than physical. It reduces mental fatigue and tension and tends to increase self-confidence. Exercise provides the satisfaction of participating with other people, an important factor in retirement.

For this reason, a pleasant way to exercise is through social sports like tennis and golf. If you play such games now, don't give them up, even if you have to play at a slower pace. If you are now inactive, start doing something that keeps your body moving and puts you in contact with others.

Many people don't involve themselves in physical activity because they feel it is too late to begin. But the body is a remarkable machine and will respond quickly to healthy habits and exercise no matter what your age. Even if you are a smoker, your lungs will immediately begin to regenerate once you stop smoking and start exercising.

The amount of exercise you should do depends on your personal physical condition, so get a checkup and ask your doctor what type of exercise would be best. The poorer your condition, the slower you must go initially until your body gradually gets accustomed to the extra effort.

In conclusion, a good doctor's rule of thumb to remember about all your body parts, both external and internal, is: use them properly or lose them.

Eat Right

Nutritional needs change as people age. In fact, you should eat ten fewer calories per day every year you get older. The reason older people get fat is they don't adjust their caloric intake. (Many also eat to relieve boredom.) The average thirty-year-old female needs about 2,200 calories a day. The average seventy-year-old only 1,700 a day.

If you get fat you run two or three times the risk of heart disease as a person of normal weight. Being overweight can also increase surgical risks and complicate existing diseases. If you overeat because you're bored, take a walk, visit friends. Don't just eat to kill time. Consult a doctor about a proper diet, and follow it. (You can also get a lot of free diet information from the Food and Drug Administration, 5600 Fishers Way, Rockville, Maryland 20852. Other information and services on various health organizations are available in Appendix C.)

PHYSICAL AND MENTAL CHANGES OF AGING

Some aspects of aging are inevitable; others are not.

There are some normal body changes we all experience as we grow older. For instance, height gradually decreases because of the years of compression of the soft discs between the vertebrae of the spine. But through exercise, walking, and sitting erect, you can minimize the pressure on the vertebral discs and retard the shrinking process.

As already mentioned, body weight will increase by about 10 percent because of the natural increase in the overall proportion of body fat, changes in metabolism and physical activity, and a corresponding decrease in the amount of calories needed to perform physical functions.

Another natural consequence of aging is that bones become more fragile because of a natural loss of calcium, so you should include foods in your diet that are a good source of calcium. Also joints may tend to be less limber. The ligaments connecting them shorten and lose their elasticity, and the natural lubricating fluid of the joints diminishes. Starting an exercise program now will help minimize that stiffness—another good reason to make exercise a regular part of your life.

Digestion changes with age. The stomach may shrink slightly, and there may be a reduced ability to absorb nutrients through the intestines. You can offset this problem and aid your entire digestive system by paying attention to the foods you eat. The earlier you begin lessening the assaults on your stomach with junk food and alcohol, the better you'll feel when you get older.

Heart and lungs don't function as efficiently owing to the natural formation of fibrous and fatty tissues. Much of this decline is caused by lack of exercise—which you can do something about.

Many people, including doctors, assume older people experience diminished mental powers and are more susceptible to mental illness. Both are untrue. Mental powers remain relatively unchanged, although the old do experience a loss of short-term memory. As for mental illness, the problem is often improper diagnosis of their condition. According to a recent study in the psychiatric division of New York's Bellevue Hospital, 71 out of 116 newly admitted patients over sixty-five did not have psychological disorders but were suffering from medical problems that manifested themselves as mental problems. In many cases, the mental disorders disappeared when the disease itself was treated.

Dr. Robert Butler, head of the National Institute on Aging in Bethesda, Maryland, says: "The failure to diagnose and treat reversible brain syndrome (temporary incapacity of the brain) is so unnecessary and yet so widespread that I would caution families of older persons to question doctors involved in care about this." The causes could be malnutrition and anemia, dehydration, infection, drugs, head injuries, congestive heart failure, reaction to surgery, among many others.

But if you decrease your activity and involvement in retirement, depression could creep up on you before you know it. Symptoms include sleeplessness, loss of appetite, unaccountable weight loss, constipation, and a general feeling of fatigue. Depression is common and curable. The simplest remedy is to stay active and involved.

Combating Loneliness and Depression

People who become mentally inactive or depressed develop physical ailments more rapidly than do people who remain mentally active. Physicians and psychologists today are almost unanimous in their belief that mental well-being promotes good physical health.

Why is it then that depression visits retirees at a rate higher than any other segment of the population? Let's take a look at some of the reasons.

A number of years ago, two psychologists developed what has become known as a "life change index." This is a ranking of stress-causing incidents in life. These are not only disaster situations that we would all immediately recognize as causes of stress but also good things such as promotions, marital reconciliations, or vacations. Of the first thirty-one items on this list, over a third are highly likely to occur to the retiree, such as change in working hours, living conditions, in work responsibilities, in financial state. In addition, since people retire at an age when illness becomes more frequent, a number of the stress factors that relate to personal injury (such as death of friends or family) are also inherent in the life of the senior. It's little wonder then that depression hits retirees at a rate higher than that of any other segment of the population.

Surviving the Death of a Spouse

A primary cause of depression among the retired is often the death of a spouse. My wife died when I was sixty-seven, and the grief and depression that followed at first seemed intolerable. In most cases, the first to go will be the husband. The problem for the wife, then, becomes how to survive emotionally. If you have a friend who loses a spouse, the best thing you can do is offer your continued friendship and support. Your friend doesn't need a date, just companionship and time to adjust.

There are, however, some concrete things you can do to confront that situation before it arises. First, you can let your spouse know that you would encourage him or her to seek companionship of both sexes after you are gone. I know that is easier said than done, but loneliness will be your spouse's burden, not yours. In the event of your death, your friends and relatives will most likely show great concern and affection for about a year. Your survivor may even be invited to live with one of the children for a time, if there are children. But ultimately the survivor will be on his or her own. Some people are fortunate enough to find companionship again. Older women often move in together for this reason. But there will be considerable difficulty at first adjusting to the new role of being a single person, and it won't be helped by the fact that members of the same sex in your circle of friends may regard your spouse as a threat to their marriages. (Old people are no different from young people; they still jealously guard what they have.) The point is to anticipate all this.

Another valuable idea for a couple is to encourage the self-sufficiency of each other. The satisfaction that comes from knowing you are capable of performing small tasks by yourself helps greatly to reduce the fear and depression of surviving your spouse—without even considering how much easier life becomes for both of you as a result. Make sure he or she knows how to do simple things, like driving a car. I know many widows who have cars in their garages but don't know how to drive. Now they are too afraid to learn.

Try to prepare your spouse to be self-reliant around the house. If you know how to fix minor plumbing problems, light switches, sticky windows and door locks, instruct your partner as you perform the repairs. If you are a good cook, pass on some of your skills. And be willing to learn from your partner for your own sake. Acquiring new skills and knowledge create a greater sense of satisfaction and self-confidence, which can combat depression and loneliness, help you help others, and keep you healthily involved.

BE INVOLVED, STAY INVOLVED

Don't retire from life.

Many retirement books tell people to stay involved, to retire from a job but not from life. Certainly that's good advice. But too frequently it comes too late, for retirement from life has taken place prior to retirement from the job. What happens is that as they grow older many people drop—or, even worse, fail to take up—community involvement activities which would immeasurably increase their sense of participation in the active world once they retire.

They become onlookers, spectators, while the rest of society operates as usual. As a consequence, once they retire they suffer a terrible loss of self-esteem and a feeling of helplessness, which worsen because of declining income.

If you are now in your forties or fifties, you have a great deal to offer civic clubs, charities, political and professional organizations, and community clubs of all kinds. Those in which you participate now will continue to welcome your participation long after you have retired from your job. There's no mandatory retirement age from these clubs.

Professional organizations particularly are worth joining. They benefit you during your active working years, as well as later when you retire and want consulting work or even part-time employment. These are the very places where that potential can be fully explored.

Start cultivating an interest in a hobby now no matter what it is—reading, gardening, golf, visiting museums, or whatever. Join a chess club, stamp club, or magicians' group. Participate in political, religious, civic, or service groups. Volunteer your services at hospitals, schools, the Braille Institute. You can find these organizations and groups everywhere. One of the great advantages to them is their national character. Even if you retire to another town you will still be welcomed at the local branch of the organization. They also often offer special benefits such as medical plans or reduced group travel rates.

Do whatever interests you. The result will be relief from boredom, and you will gain participation, involvement, and health.

One magazine found that many outstanding historians, philosophers, botanists, geologists, and inventors made more significant contributions to society while in their seventies, eighties, and nineties than they did in their thirties. Maggie Kuhn was sixty-four when she organized the Gray Panthers, the nationwide group of senior activists. Gandhi was seventy-two when he led India's independence movement.

Grandma Moses didn't begin painting until she was seventy-four. Golda Meir was seventy-five when she led Israel as Prime Minister. Jomo Kenyatta was in his seventies when he became the first president of the African Republic of Kenya.

Albert Schweitzer lectured around the world on the brotherhood of man when he was in his eighties. Artur Rubinstein is still recording and playing brilliant piano in his eighties. George Burns won an Oscar for his role in *The Sunshine Boys* the same year he turned eighty. And Bertrand Russell, one of the most influential thinkers of the twentieth century, was ninety when he intervened with heads of state during the Cuban-American missile crisis.

Ben Franklin gave some good advice when he was eighty: "Keep up your spirits and that will keep up your bodies." It's still well worth remembering.

MEDICARE AND OTHER HEALTH INSURANCE

Medicare covers less than you think.

You must have health insurance when you go into retirement. Without it you could go broke paying medical bills. Before retirement, you may be adequately covered by a company group plan. That won't help if you can't take that plan into retirement with you. Check it out. You may be shocked to discover that your policy may be terminated the day you retire, leaving you without adequate health insurance at a time in life when you need it the most. Health insurance companies seem to be in business to protect young people, who seldom get sick, not to protect older people who need the insurance more often.

If you are counting on Medicare, the federal government insurance you qualify for automatically when you are sixty-

five, you'd better count again. After we look at what it will
and won't do for you, we'll discuss government and private
policies that help supplement its inadequacies.

The Great Retirement Lie has led most people to believe
that once they reach sixty-five, the government's Medicare
health insurance program will cover all their medical bills.
That is simply untrue. Medicare covers only about a third to
a half of the average retiree's medical bills. According to
Consumer Reports, "The average yearly medical bill for
someone over sixty-five is $1,218. Of that, Medicare pays
only $463." The government proudly tells us that Medicare
pays for 80 percent of most normal medical bills. That
sounds good. But when you figure in all the exclusions, the
medicines and illnesses that are exempt from coverage, the
net result is that, depending on what figures you use,
*Medicare pays for only 38 to 50 percent of the medical bills
of the retired.*

Medicare does pay for about 80 percent of the "covered"
costs after you pay a certain deductible. This varies according to the service. "Covered" costs mean that Medicare may
determine that it should cost $15 for your medical service,
even though your doctor may charge you $40. So you have
a choice: you either make up the difference yourself or find
a cheaper doctor. Since the enactment of Medicare in 1966,
the gap between runaway health costs and what Medicare
actually covers has steadily widened. *Consumer Reports*
states that, at the time they studied it, Medicare paid only
62 percent of the hospital bills and only 52 percent of the
"covered" doctor bills. Older persons in nursing homes
fared even worse: only *3.3 percent* of their expenses were
paid.

There are a lot of things Medicare does not cover. It does
not pay for long-term illnesses, preventive medical care,
out-of-hospital prescription drugs, hearing aids, eyeglasses,
dental work, and many other things.

Actually, Medicare was never intended to be a comprehensive health plan for seniors. It was to aid, not completely

cover, the retired, who are the part of the population most hard pressed by rising health costs. You would be well advised to study, before you get there, what Medicare will and will not do for you in retirement.

Medicare has two parts. Part A is hospital insurance, which is free once you reach age sixty-five, whether or not you retire. Part B is voluntary supplemental medical insurance and costs about $8 a month.

Part A pays for a semi-private hospital room, regular nursing services, X-rays, operating-room fees, and the use of such hospital equipment as a wheelchair. The coverage extends for a maximum hospital stay of sixty days. You must pay an initial deductible fee of about $125. From the sixty-first through ninetieth day of hospitalization, you must pay the first approximate $30 a day for the services just described and Medicare pays the rest. From the ninety-first through one-hundred-fiftieth day, you pay the first approximate $60 a day and Medicare pays the rest.

As you can see, Medicare operates on sixty-day benefit periods. Naturally, if your stay is longer than sixty days, it gets expensive. The only way to avoid the higher deductibles is to leave the hospital before your sixtieth day and stay out for sixty more consecutive days. If you do that, you may reenter the hospital and start on a new "initial" sixty-day benefit period, which would cost you only the $125 deductible. If you can't manage to keep out of the hospital the required sixty days and are in and out for short periods that add up to sixty days or more, you must then move up to the next benefit level where, as I stated, you must begin paying the deductible of $30 a day. Once you reach ninety days of hospitalization, you go to yet another level of coverage, called the Lifetime Reserve Period, and pay $60 a day until your one-hundred-fiftieth day of hospitalization. Every Medicare recipient had only sixty days in the Lifetime Reserve Period. Once it's used up, it's gone for good.

Part A does not pay for television, telephone, or private duty nurses. Except in emergencies, benefits are paid only to those hospitals participating in the Medicare program.

Part B is the major medical. If you wait more than a year after your sixty-fifth birthday to voluntarily enroll in Part B (everyone sixty-five and over is eligible), you will be charged a higher premium than the normal cost of approximately $8 a month. The premium goes up about 10 percent for each year you delay in enrolling.

Part B covers the major portion of a doctor's medical and surgical bills, no matter where the services are performed. It also pays for part of the expense of diagnostic tests, ambulance service, X-rays, artificial eyes and limbs, and emergency-room treatment.

You must pay the initial deductible of about $75 each calendar year. Medicare then pays 80 percent of what they call "reasonable" charges, and you pay the rest. If your doctor charges more than the amount designated by Medicare as "reasonable" for his services, you will end up with a chunk of the bill. More information on the coverage you receive from Parts A and B of Medicare is listed in the many free pamphlets available at your local Social Security office.

If it's your intention to rely solely on Medicare in retirement, the effects could be devastating. I know, because not a day passes that I don't hear from some retired person needing help in getting medical treatment. The scenario is usually the same: The necessary treatment is too costly and Medicare doesn't cover much of the bill. Dr. Butler bears this out: "Physicians have become more and more selective about their patients, and people on Medicaid and Medicare often have found themselves unwelcome at private doctors' offices and at private voluntary hospitals." Butler also states that "Older patients have difficulty when they need hospitalization unless they have a regular doctor and, generally speaking, a good-sized income. When they become ill, a significant number of them arrive at the emergency room of voluntary nonprofit and public hospitals to discover that they are not considered desirable patients."

Medicaid

If your medical expenses become too burdensome to pay, you may be eligible for Medicaid, which is a federal-state program designed to offer medical assistance to low-income people. Medicaid appears under various names, depending on the state, but you may apply for it at your local welfare office. Don't be afraid to ask about it. Just as the taxes taken out of your salary during your working years entitle you to Social Security and Medicare benefits, you are also entitled to Medicaid. The same is true of all other programs funded by the taxes the government collected from you. Some people have the peculiar belief that they're receiving a public handout if they go on welfare. If you're an older American, you've probably paid enough taxes in your lifetime to own the building the local office operates in.

Senior citizens who are on the Supplemental Security Income (SSI) program I discussed earlier are automatically eligible for free Medicaid hospital and doctor care, which includes doctor visits, hospital stays, dental work, prescriptions, and other medical services.

There's a special type of medical welfare funding called Medically Needed Only (MNO). Most people have never heard of this, but you're eligible to collect even if you have a more expensive house and car than the normal welfare guidelines specify. It's for the not-so-poor retired who are facing extraordinary medical expenses. The key to obtaining MNO is to apply for it *before* you incur the medical expenses. If you or your husband or wife find you must enter a hospital for expensive medical treatment, apply for MNO immediately. If you wait until you're out of the hospital and start receiving bills, you're out of luck. MNO is not retroactive.

PRIVATE HEALTH INSURANCE

Investigate thoroughly, buy early, and buy enough. Then stay healthy.

To pay for what Medicare does not provide, you must see that you have supplemental private health insurance policies, otherwise expenses from a major illness could easily wipe you out. It is estimated that about half of all retired persons have one or more private health insurance policies, in addition to Medicare. Don't be in the half that doesn't.

Unfortunately, policies to cover most of what Medicare doesn't under Part B are expensive and hard to get for those already retired. The least expensive way to handle this is by buying one of the supplemental plans specifically designed to fill in the gaps in Medicare. Their cost doesn't increase with your age. Such plans won't protect you in the event of long-term illness, but they will usually cover Medicare deductibles—the 20 percent that Part B of Medicare does not cover—as well as part of the daily room charges you would otherwise incur with a hospital stay of more than sixty days.

The supplemental policies differ from area to area. Blue Cross/Blue Shield is a good place to start investigating. Their "65 Special" is a reasonable plan. The Guardian Life Insurance Company and Mutual of Omaha also have moderately priced plans. Other supplemental plans are available through the National Council of Senior Citizens (NCSC) and the American Association of Retired Persons (AARP). Each company or organization has several supplemental options.

Most of the Medicare supplements do not cover out-of-hospital prescription drugs, so to have your prescriptions filled inexpensively, you might consider the Pharmacy

Service of AARP. To be eligible, you must be fifty-five and pay a $3 membership fee. But it is worth it. The address is AARP, P.O. Box 199, Long Beach, California 90801.

The best way to assure your own coverage is to start buying adequate health insurance while you're still working full time. Since you are young enough, you are a better risk for the insurance company so you have a wider latitude in choosing your policy, making it easier for you to get the health insurance plan you want. If you investigate carefully, you should be able to find a policy with provisions you can take into retirement with you.

Finding the insurance plan that is right for you is not easy. Part of the problem is that there are more than 1,200 separate health insurance plans available in the United States. Many of them are filled with all kinds of exclusions and deductibles. But there are some basic ways to proceed when buying health insurance, whether you are still working or already retired.

When shopping for health insurance, the first thing is to make sure you buy from a financially sound, dependable company. You may have the best insurance policy, but it's useless if the company is unable to pay off when you file your claim. To ascertain the financial strength of a company, consult *Best's Insurance Reports* at your library. Best's ratings, in descending order, are: "most substantial," "very substantial," "substantial," and "considerable." Investigate only companies that have "most substantial" and "very substantial" ratings. An exception to this advice would be Blue Cross and Blue Shield. Although they are not included in Best's ratings, they are considered sound companies and are among those that offer good policies if they are available in your state.

You should also check to see that your prospective insurance company is responsive to claims with quick, courteous, and fair service. You don't want to have to chase them for the money to pay your medical bills. Although this kind of information is not easy to track down, you might ask your

insurance salesman for names of a few customers who have
insurance with the company and contact them to see how
they have fared.

If you are buying an individual plan rather than participating in a group plan, the choice of an agent is important
because he is the one with whom you must deal. My
experience has been that it's safest not to buy from an agent
who works for only one insurance company. Such a person
is bound to be prejudiced in favor of his own company,
whether or not the company is any good, because the agent
is dependent on the sales commissions from that company
for his livelihood.

So the best choice for an insurance agent would be one
who works for an independent agency or a broker who
represents more than one company and more than one line
of insurance. These agencies are independent contractors
and can afford to operate for the benefit of the consumer.
Independent agencies are also strong enough to help policy-
holders, especially with regard to claims.

The thing to be most wary of is mail-order insurance
that is sold with the aid of million-dollar advertising
campaigns. These companies have traditionally denied
payment on a greater percentage of claims than have
other companies.

Getting the Right Coverage

To get all the coverage you should have, you'll probably
need at least two different policies or one policy that has
two facets to it: a broad hospital, medical, and surgical
policy; and a major medical policy. *Hospital, medical, and
surgical* is a basic plan that pays for your hospital room and
the in-hospital services of doctor and surgeons. A good
policy will pay for nearly all the services you receive while
you're in the hospital, whether it was illness or accident that
put you there.

Major medical coverage is back-up coverage for your hospital, medical, and surgical plan. It pays for costly illnesses and accidents that outrun the coverage of the basic plan. Major medical plans usually come with a deductible and pay a certain percentage, normally about 80 percent of the bill.

Your insurance policies will pay you either "service benefits" or "indemnity benefits." Service benefits are the best because they pay no matter how much inflation has increased the cost of the service since you purchased the policy. Indemnity benefits pay a fixed amount of money. If your policy pays an indemnity benefit of $50 a day while you are in the hospital, and the hospital rates go up to $80 a day, you make up the difference. A service benefit, on the other hand, covers the increased costs.

In addition, you want a broad-coverage policy, not one with a lot of exclusions. You don't want to leave the hospital with a stack of bills nor do you want to accept lower quality medical care because of poor coverage. For example, you don't want a policy that covers you against only one specific disease, such as cancer. Your policy should cover a broad range of illnesses, since you can't know in advance what illness you may get. Furthermore, you should be sure your policy covers prescription drugs and diagnostic tests both in and out of the hospital. You may also want a policy that covers dental care and nursing-home care.

Make sure your coverage is substantial as well as broad and covers the full amount of services. If your operation is going to cost $800, you don't want your coverage to stop at $600.

When it comes to an important matter like health insurance, it is foolish not to investigate the market thoroughly. Take your time. By shopping around you can often discover a better health insurance policy at a lower cost. Insurance is like anything else you buy. If you settle for the first thing you find, you may pay too high a price and get a poor deal. Besides, policy coverages differ from state to state, often from community to community. For instance, Blue Cross in New York is not the same as Blue Cross in Oregon.

Converting Group Plans into Individual Plans

Group plans are usually cheaper and offer better coverage than individual plans. In addition, there are fewer exclusions and limitations in group plans, you rarely have to provide detailed information about your health, or take a physical before you qualify. If you can get good group coverage now, get it, but make sure you are in a plan that has a conversion clause that gives you the right to convert to a guaranteed-renewable individual policy without giving evidence of insurability. The last thing you want is to end up retiring from a job and losing your insurance without a chance to convert to an individual policy with no strings attached. Your premiums with conversion privileges will be a bit higher, but that's the price you must pay. And it is a price well worth paying.

There are two more important questions you should ask: (1) Can your policy be canceled because of age? If so, at what age? (2) Can premiums be raised because of age? If so, how much? If you look carefully, you can find guaranteed-renewable policies, no matter what age you reach.

Buyer, Beware!

There are a few cautions about medical insurance plans. First, watch out for waiting periods. If you buy an individual policy, it may have a clause about a waiting period during which it will not cover certain illnesses or conditions that you had when you took out the policy. Such waiting periods for preexisting conditions should be limited to a year or less.

Some policies have waiting periods for coverage of new illnesses. Some waiting periods last as long as six months for coverage of specific illnesses, such as a heart attack. The shorter the waiting period, the better. Other policies cover you immediately. Some policies have exclusionary riders that limit coverage for you in important areas, so read the brochure fully. If you can't get rid of the riders that are denying you the coverage you need, don't buy the policy.

Second, don't get insurance poor. As important as it is to secure your retirement by being adequately covered by health insurance, there is a limit as to how much you should buy. Some retired people worry themselves sick over whether or not they have enough. One woman I know has seven different health policies, each one overlapping the next. She is wasting a lot of money simply because the policies are poorly coordinated.

Some people think that by having such overlapping coverage with different companies they will be able to make a profit on their illnesses. Let me tell you that it is a tough way to make money and, by and large, it doesn't happen. In most cases if one policy pays for your medical expenses the company that holds the other policy to cover that particular expense will not pay you as well. In fact, when you take out new policies today, you must tell the new company about existing coverage. The two companies then get together to make sure that they are not both paying for the same illness.

The big danger in worrying too much about insurance is that you will end up buying every policy in the insurance agent's book, whether you need it or not. So my advice is: decide what coverage you really need, then buy no more. You've done all you can in this area. Now follow your common sense and plan to stay healthy.

**PLAN TO FIGHT:
A Short Course
in Senior Advocacy**

*Seniors are potentially the most powerful voting bloc
in the nation.*

Americans often seem oblivious to anything over sixty-
five years old unless it is found on an antique dealer's shelf.
So if you are in your forties or fifties, you may be tempted
to skip this chapter in the belief that senior advocacy is still
a long way from affecting your life.

That is far from the truth. Today's retired are not the
only losers in a society that seems hostile to their needs.
Younger generations will inherit what is now condoned.
If you, the nonretired, passively accept the climate in
which today's retired must struggle for survival, then
you, the future retired, will deserve that inheritance. In
twenty years or less you, too, may find yourself poor
and powerless.

My point is simple. From the first page of this book, I
have been urging you to begin now to secure your financial
future, your health, and your continuing participation in
society. If I can also convince you now to become an
advocate for senior causes it may help you achieve a more
comfortable existence at the time you begin your own
retirement.

This chapter is directed toward both those under sixty-five, who have a stake in creating a better future, and those already retired, who have an even higher stake in getting their present needs met.

The retired of today helped form this country. They sacrificed their sons during four wars, brought the country out of the greatest depression in its history, and created the technological and medical achievements that have made the nation one of the most affluent in the world. Yet they have inherited very little of what they created.

So the question becomes, what can they do today to regain the comfort, power, and influence they so clearly deserve? The solution is clear, for their struggle is little different from the struggle for equality of other underprivileged groups. The retired must become strong advocates for themselves. There will be no adequate solutions to their economic and social problems until they and their future counterparts begin working together and fighting for their own cause.

The only way for the retired to reclaim their fair share of the economic wealth is to reach out and take it. They now have the numerical strength to make government responsive to their needs. It's time to wake up and grab the opportunity. Every economic benefit obtained for the retired today is a benefit banked for the retired of the future. The more social and economic good gained now to aid the retired, the more humane and comfortable will be the climate for the person who retires in ten or twenty years. And the way to achieve it is through senior advocacy.

SENIOR ADVOCACY

The retired person's life is controlled by people who are not retired.

Advocacy simply means being vocal, visible, and forceful in support of a cause. It begins at home, in the community, by following the strategy of any successful political campaign with national goals. And it means applying the same principles that seniors have used for forty-plus years in business and other pursuits: clearly outlined objectives, a strategy for reaching them, determination, and unflagging effort.

Senior advocacy does not begin with calling a news conference in front of the statehouse. It begins with knocking on doors. The more supporters for your cause, the more widespread your influence.

Every organized group that gets its way in this society does it by getting a lot of people together and then going out and lobbying their point of view—before the city council, school board, or whatever agency has the power to finance programs important to them. But retired people have not been doing much of that. Seldom do they go before city councils to make requests. Rarely do they petition local government for needed services. In community after community, seniors just haven't taken advantage of age power, except for a few isolated cases where the Gray Panthers and other senior activist groups have interceded on behalf of their cause. (For a complete listing of senior organizations, see Appendix D.)

But they must begin, for the retired person's life is controlled by people who are not retired. The ones who devise Social Security and Medicare programs, who advise the retired on how to live, who are charged by the government and the private sector with running the affairs of the retired often have little idea of what being retired means. Only those who are already retired can best judge their needs. And those who still have some years to go should help them.

IF YOU WANT TO HAVE AN
IMPACT—ORGANIZE

On being loud.

If you haven't dropped in on a meeting of one of your local government bodies, you should. At the top of its agenda are matters of importance to the special-interest groups who lobby for their causes. At the bottom are the petitions of private citizens who have not yet organized themselves into lobbying groups. This is usually where most senior citizens fall. At the bottom.

To have an impact on city councils and other official agencies whose decisions can affect your life, you must organize. Organized groups—those that have the strength of numbers or money—are high-priority business for these agencies. Groups with few supporters and little money are low-priority.

Why do you suppose building contractors, land developers, and other big businesses take up most of the time of your local government? They have the power, either in numbers, money, or both. The retired, on the other hand, have traditionally never organized, never recruited supporters, nor otherwise shown that they represent a substantial economic and political bloc within the community. As a result, their causes have received little attention and even less action.

All governing bodies pay attention to the loudest voices. So be loud. If you advocate loud enough and long enough and show the strength of numbers, you'll get what you want. Otherwise, you'll get nothing.

KNOW YOUR POLITICAL POWER

Making government responsive to your needs.

In general, politicians are uninformed about seniors and rarely appeal to the senior vote. They are insensitive to the needs of the retired, just as they are often insensitive to the needs of other underprivileged groups in the community. To capture the attention of these politicians, the retired need a sense of just how important they are to a community, so that they can go about advocating their causes more effectively and confidently.

Here are some facts the politicians and you should know. First of all, the retired population is the most powerful voting bloc in the nation. Although seniors comprise only about 11 percent of the nation's population, 90 percent of them are registered voters and 65 percent vote regularly. This means that retired people comprise at least *25 percent of the vote* cast in any election. That could be a great big power bloc. That 25 percent, coupled with the support of sympathetic voters in other age groups, is enough to kick any public official out of office or put any aspiring public servant in. It is enough clout to approve or defeat any ballot measure or referendum.

At the grass-roots level, if retired seniors voted as a bloc they could determine who would sit on the city councils, or any other agency elected by the public. At the national level, the senior population could elect or defeat any candidate. Yet during the 1976 Democratic and Republican national conventions, I did not hear one appeal by the major presidential candidates to the senior vote. Politicians have come to believe that apathy to public affairs by the retired is a fact of life. But by the time you finish reading this chapter you will be equipped to change the apathetic attitude of politicians as well as the apathy of the retired in your community.

THE RETIRED ARE PROFITABLE BUSINESS

Social and economic gains for the retired are often gains for the whole community.

Besides being a powerful voting bloc, retired people are the most profitable business in almost any town. Indeed, without them many communities would likely go broke. Even poor seniors on welfare are a financial asset to their community. Most people, including the retired themselves, probably don't know that.

Let's take my area of Ventura County as an example. It has more than 40,000 seniors, an average number for an area of its size. Welfare regulations state that every person sixty-five or older is entitled to an income of at least $276 per month. An estimated 10,000 seniors in Ventura County live on that amount; the rest have a higher income. The overall average is a little over $5,000 per year. Forty thousand seniors times $5,000 equals $200,000,000! That's the amount retired people pour into the local economy, and that's a lot of economic power. And since Ventura County is largely an agricultural area, it stands to reason that if you live in a suburban or urban area, the retired population may be contributing not millions, but billions of dollars to the local economy.

If the retired were suddenly to move out of almost any community, that community would likely go bankrupt. I've made that statement dozens of times to business groups I've spoken to. Some of the young business people challenge me, claiming that the retired are more of a drain on the community than a boon. They cite social programs the community must provide—senior recreation centers, adult day-care centers, and the like. They talk about the need to provide public transportation, utilities, and other services.

There are four things these business people don't know:

1. They don't realize that about 80 percent of the money to establish and run senior services at the local level is paid for by the *federal* government. That federal money is specifically earmarked for senior services and would go to some other community if the home community did not apply for it.

2. Federal money also comes into the communities in the form of Social Security checks. When the retired person cashes that check and buys groceries and food, the grocer then pays employees, who in turn buy gas or clothes at local shops. The shops pay their help, who then are able to buy their own food, gas, or clothes— and so on. Eventually, the money leaves the commu-

nity when goods are purchased from an outside company that takes its profits out of the area. It is important to realize that federal money coming into the community becomes "money-in-action," that is, money that buys things or pays salaries. Money-in-action creates the wealth on which a community thrives.

3. Social and economic gains for the retired are usually gains for the younger population as well. Take the public transit system. This is one of the prime needs of retired people in most areas. Many of them are eventually deprived of their drivers' licenses because of strict auto licensing laws. But, in addition to aiding seniors, public transit systems would also aid children going to school and workers who have no access to cars or carpools in an automobile-congested city. What's more, public transit systems would help alleviate air pollution—a problem for nearly every city in the country.

4. Finally, retired people are now often paying more than their share for utilities and other services. Usually people who put out one trash barrel are charged the same rate as people who put out four. People who use $2 worth of electricity are charged the electric company's minimum rate of $7 or $8. This should be changed.

WHAT IS A SENIOR ADVOCATE?

A fighter for the cause.

Anyone can support a senior advocate who surfaces in a community, but not everyone can be an activist because not all have the health, time, energy, or assertive personality necessary to wage a war of words with politicians and bureaucrats. The best advocate is also someone who is lucky enough to have sufficient income to be reasonably free from the worries of daily survival. Of course, he or she must be aggressive, otherwise not much will get done. The active senior advocate must be willing to take risks, for he or she can become a target of abuse from those threatened by the tactics used. The advocate must be thick-skinned enough so that verbal attacks bounce off.

Like anyone disturbing the status quo, I have had a lot of run-ins with officials myself. Less than a year after I was hired by the county as senior citizens coordinator there was talk of firing me. Some officials publicly criticized me as "bothersome" and "abrupt" for insisting that politicians do something for the retired. One even suggested that my "crusade for the retired" would backfire and that my appeals before the county's governing bodies would become a matter of public amusement.

But what these officials didn't realize was that I wasn't speaking just for myself. I was simply one retired person articulating the needs and desires of thousands of others in the same community. The retired persons' movement in Ventura County is now in full swing and many more senior advocates are fighting for our causes.

THE BUILDING BLOCKS OF STRATEGY

Using the organized strength in the retired community to achieve your goals.

No matter what your age, if you want to become a senior advocate, there are a number of steps to follow to achieve your goals. Here is a short "handbook" of suggestions on strategy for senior advocates, distilled from my own experiences of fighting city hall the last few years.

Enlist Support

Rather than fighting as one person, enlist the support of self-starters scattered throughout the community. You'll

find them everywhere. Check especially in your local newspapers where community-level advocates receive the most
exposure. Others can be found in the audience of city
council meetings, the so-called "city hall watchers" who
make a hobby of keeping an eye on the activities of the city
council. Or you might strike up a conversation with someone in a park and discover another enthusiastic supporter or
leader.

You'll find energetic supporters and co-advocates in
many of the senior clubs, such as the Forty-Plus Club, the
Golden Age Club, the Friendship Club, the Friendly Club,
the Leisure Club, and local branches of the American Association of Retired Persons. They are in nearly every city and
town. These clubs all have individual members who keep
things moving with their enthusiasm and ideas. Some may
be former union members who used organized advocacy in
their younger years to gain employee benefits. The approach they used is the same approach you'll need to obtain
retirement goals. So get to know them. In addition, if you
can achieve cooperation among the numerous retirement
clubs in your area, you'll have the backing of an army to
help you fight for your objectives.

In my town there are about 6,000 retired persons.
With phone calls to a few key people, I can set a senior
grapevine in operation that will summon a thousand retired persons within a few hours. That's organization.
That's cooperation.

Get the Momentum Going

Once you have enlisted your core of retired persons, both
as supporters and co-advocates, begin to make your presence and cause known throughout the community. There
are a number of ways to do this. Offer yourselves as speakers at clubs. Write letters to the editors of local newspapers.
Talk to reporters at newspapers and local radio stations.

Although many people may want to help in the accomplish-
ment of a worthy goal, they first have to understand the
cause before they can support it.

While you are going about promoting your cause, you
should be aware that a catchy name goes a long way toward
furthering its exposure. The press loves a catchy title. It also
helps create a memorable image in the public's eye. For
example, once I tried to persuade the local county government to free some funds that would provide needy seniors
with pets at no cost. I formed a small advocacy group and
called it the Sad Dog Committee. The name caught the eye
of several reporters, and their stories did the trick. Another
time, while trying to generate donations of gardening imple-
ments to help a senior club gardening project, I told the
news media we were reviving the Victory Gardens of World
War II. The term "Victory Gardens" was what the news
media needed to write the feature stories we wanted. On a
broader advocacy level, Maggie Kuhn's "Gray Panthers" is a
hard name to forget.

Establish Priorities

If you have the support of a number of senior clubs, each
will have its own view of what the highest priority should
be, so divide your goals among the groups involved. Assign
each group one top priority as well as a number of lesser
objectives. One group may be in charge of advocating a
public transit system, but its members should be available to
offer support to another group fighting for a free medical
clinic for the elderly. The support should be in the form of
a show of strength when the proposal for the free clinic
comes before the city council and also in the form of
volunteers to help with publicity.

With this kind of organization, you can advocate a dozen
objectives at once and stand a good chance of gaining them
all, because you have a large base of strength.

Get Your Facts Straight

After you have determined your objectives and enlisted your support, the next step is to do some serious homework. Make sure you have a proposal worth considering. What you don't know can hurt you. Gather all the facts and statistics you need. Make sure you understand all the issues involved and can give an intelligent answer to any questions you may be asked. Talk with others in the community who might be sympathetic. Of special value are experts who can give you hard information, and knowledgeable seniors who can give you sound advice, because they are the ones who know the most about senior needs. (Statistical data to support your request can be gotten from the census records at city hall and at the library.)

Get Your Proposal in Order

Once you're convinced that you have gathered enough information and thoroughly understand the issue, the next step is to make an effective presentation.

What you say to the city council is certainly important, but how you say it is equally so. Write your proposal in clear, straightforward language. Rehearse your pitch before you actually deliver it by practicing out loud at home. Aim for a clear, firm voice, much as the tone you used with your children when you were one step away from letting them have it on the backside. You want to be sure the council understands you are determined and will use all the organized strength in the communtiy to achieve your goals.

Work with City Hall

Whether you call it a city council, board of selectmen, or any other name, the local governing body is where to start advocating. But you can't simply run into a city council meeting and start shouting your demands. They'll either throw you out or listen with a deaf ear and tap impatiently on the table. Either way, you won't accomplish much.

You need an organized approach. Contact your city council for literature available on how meetings are conducted and how matters for discussion get on the council agenda. Play the game by their rules. It generally works if you take the time to understand the rules first and if you are persistent.

Make a Show of Strength

When your proposal comes up on the city council agenda, pack the audience with as many members of your supporting groups as possible. Seat them up front. Be obvious and huge. It will serve notice to council members that they are not dealing with only a few isolated people but a big bloc, and it will give the person who presents the proposal the moral support he or she needs. Since groups of advocates appearing before a governing body definitely do influence the decision the governing body makes, keep the group coming back until the council acts favorably.

During an austerity drive at the local community college in my area, the administration was talking about cutting out some "senior economic survival" courses. They were thinking of it, that is, until I arranged to have fifty retired people present at the college board meeting when the "cutting out" was to take place. The college officials—a group who are elected, not appointed—took one look at that mass of old faces and announced that the senior programs would continue.

There is yet another way of showing strength. If you read of a person advocating a cause that would be beneficial to retired persons, write a letter to the city council or other governing body responsible for making the decision. Get others to write as well. The politicians estimate that every letter received by a governing body represents the opinion of 1,000 constituents, since so few bother to write their elected representatives letters in support or in opposition to anything.

Keep Your Cool

Don't lose your temper, though, if the council doesn't seem interested in your proposal. Thank the members for their time and consideration. Your good conduct will leave the door open for you to return with a stronger case at a later date. If you leave a pleasant, businesslike impression, they will remember that and be more attentive when you return before them again. Losing your temper and hurling insults will make it easy for them to turn your proposal down and ignore you in future council appearances.

Stay in Contact

Keep the city officials constantly aware of your presence. You and your retirement groups should become watchdogs of the city council. Once the groups are organized, arrange it so that representatives of one of the groups are at each council meeting. By sharing the load, representatives need attend meetings only once every few weeks or so. It will make council members begin to recognize retired people as a politically potent segment of the community.

Persevere

These strategies may seem simple enough, but, of course, you will meet with other conflicts and frustrations that also need to be overcome. There may be serious disagreements among the senior clubs about which priorities are the highest or about how things should be organized. Some city councils and other governing bodies may be infuriatingly stubborn about your demands. Some of the things you ask for will cost peanuts, but the decision makers will act as if you were asking for a million dollars.

That's okay. You can't expect to have things handed to you. That's not the way things work in our society. You must work and fight for what you want. If you achieve only half of what you would like to see happen, you will have come a long way toward accomplishing your goals.

APPROACHING THE NEWS MEDIA FOR SUPPORT

You can't win without them.

The news media are the catalyst that can amass enough community support to accomplish your objective. Without them, you would continually have to go door to door to enlist support. Dealing with newspapers, radio, and television can be frustrating if you don't understand how they work. Here's a short course.

Dealing with the Press

I learned how to deal with the press the hard way. I had a news release about a senior event that I wanted to get into all the newspapers. The day before the event was scheduled, one of the four daily newspapers that serve Ventura County still had not printed the story. So I went to that newspaper, showed the news release to the editor, and said, "You know, every other paper in the county has run this story but you. Don't you care about the news?" He grabbed the release from my hand and growled, "Mr. Lamb, I've got hundreds of clubs and individuals begging me to print their releases. I was going to print yours today, but I'm not about to be ordered to do anything." He threw the news release in the wastebasket. I had violated his kingdom, by telling him he was doing a rotten job. It was the way I felt, but it didn't accomplish my goal. The editor had a right to treat me as he did.

One thing I learned is to get personally acquainted with at least one reporter at every newspaper. That way if you do something wrong, you can find out from a sympathetic insider and still have a chance of the paper's running your story.

When preparing your news release, remember the important points of any news story. Answer the *who, what, when, where, why,* and *how* of the story. Include the name and telephone number of a person the paper can reach if they have questions. Spell names correctly to avoid embarrassing the people quoted and especially the paper that prints your release. Submit your story as far in advance of the paper's required deadline as possible.

It would be ideal if you could write a news story that the paper could use as is, exactly as you wrote it, but most people are not journalists and the professionals at the paper realize that. They expect to rewrite news releases, so let them. But be certain you include all the facts and that your facts are straight. Or you might be able to find a retired newswriter who would be glad to help you in your efforts. The easier you make it on the news staff, the happier they will be to assist you in the future.

I wouldn't dream of beginning to advocate a retirement cause without finding a major role in it for newspapers to play. When I decided to start a senior advocacy class at a local college, I made certain the class would be a success by utilizing the news media to the fullest. The week before the class was to begin, I flooded the papers with news releases such as the following in the Ventura County *Star-Free Press* which drew so many seniors we had to meet in the college cafeteria, instead of the regular classroom.

WANT TO BATTLE CITY HALL AND WIN?

A county employee is going to teach a course at Moorpark College on how to win fights with local government.

The instructor will be Tony Lamb, the county's senior citizens' coordinator, and the class will be senior advocacy. It will meet at Moorpark College from 6:30 to 8:30 p.m. on Wednesdays starting this week and running to Nov. 12.

"This new approach to meeting seniors' needs and solving common problems is based on the idea that seniors can and must become a powerful political force on the local level," the course announcement says.

When you send out a news release, send it to everyone— the daily papers, the weeklies, radio and television stations. Don't play favorites. If you are to maintain good media relations, treat them all equally.

When you deal with the media, don't be afraid to suggest a story to them. If you present them with a well-thought-out, polite suggestion on how a particular plight of senior citizens could make an interesting news story, they may well appreciate and use the idea. In Ventura County the newspapers and the retired have benefited mutually. Our senior advocates have given the papers good stories, and the retired community has reaped the benefits that such exposure in the mass media brings. On one occasion, when we thought city inaction was delaying the opening of a new senior center, we told the local newspaper that seniors would play bridge on the steps of the unopened center to show their displeasure. It was winter so the senior card players were bundled up in big coats as they played bridge on the steps. The next day a front-page photograph of cold-looking seniors sitting in front of their closed senior center was all it took to push city officials into swift action, and the center opened shortly afterward.

Letters to the Editor

If you don't have personal contact with a news reporter, a letter to the editor is your next best bet. Almost all newspapers have a "Letters to the editor" section. The most effective ones printed are carefully written and researched (if the subject warrants facts) and present the retired person as a thoughtful, intelligent individual. Such letters not only alert the community to your cause, but also alert local politicians, too. Politicians are usually more responsive to printed letters than they are to letters written to them personally, (especially if the writer has deftly managed to mention the politician's name in connection with the subject). A politician realizes that a published letter will be read by thousands of voting constituents who could become active supporters of the cause, and he can't afford *not to* respond to the request.

Dealing with Radio Stations

Another important resource for mass communication is radio. Radio stations are under Federal Communications Commission pressure to perform public-service work in the community. The causes of the retired certainly fall into that category.

Several radio stations in my area offer radio time to retired persons on a regular basis. It's not prime time, but it's a great opportunity to make our voices heard.

For the past three years I have been hosting a bi-monthly talk program on a local station. It's called "Open Line," and listeners are encouraged to call in and talk with the guests I have, which include local city council members and community leaders. The program gives the retired a forum to air problems and also disseminates information important to the retirement community. It's a powerful political tool for senior advocacy.

It's a good idea to have an acknowledged spokesman for senior rights in your own area meet with the local radio station managers and ask for time for a senior citizens program or even some public-service time to be used for regular appeals and announcements of coming events.

Dealing with Television Stations

Television stations can give your cause broad exposure quickly. The best way I have found to approach TV stations is to determine the particular interests of newscasters by watching them on television, and then visiting the station and asking to see that newscaster personally. Then I ask point-blank if he or she would like to do a newscast on whatever project I have going.

Shortly after beginning the senior survival course, I simply asked a reporter for one of the Los Angeles stations if his station might be interested in televising one of the classes. I explained the significance of the course, the number of people who would be interested in it (including people in their forties and fifties), and gave him all of the information that we had accumulated. He took it to the director of the news department, who decided to give us the coverage. We got a story on the air in the third largest community in America. With preparation and perseverance, you can do the same in your area. If the first station doesn't say yes, try a second or a third. If none of them say yes immediately, go back to them again with more facts and figures at a later date. Their news needs and priorities are constantly changing and if your timing was wrong the first time, it might be right the second time.

SPEAKING OUT FOR SENIOR ADVOCACY

Influencing influential people.

The objective in public speaking is to promote the needs of retired people. When I first started advocating, I gave as many as eight talks a week. Most of them were to clubs such as Rotary, Lions, Kiwanis, Jaycees, Soroptomist, AARP groups, teachers, and church groups. I talked about whatever subject they requested but eventually turned the talk into a pitch for the needs of retired people. Even when I was asked to talk before inventors' groups or scientific organizations because of my science background, I never concluded without telling them what they could do to help the retired. I always point out the incontestable fact that they, too, will be retired someday, and it is to their benefit to help the retired of today.

Public speakers are vital in order to influence groups of people to support your objectives. Clubs like fresh speakers. Remember, there are about twenty clubs in every small city which meet weekly. That means there are openings for more than a thousand speakers a year. You could be one of them. Talk about the senior activities with which you are involved. The club members are interested in such things. Besides, they get tired of hearing speeches from the local businessmen who are usually invited.

What we have done in my area is make up a list of potential senior speakers and send them to all the clubs. You should be able to find speakers right in your own group of advocates. A potential public speaker may not even have given a speech before, but you can spot likely candidates because they generally exude self-confidence, know what they are talking about, and are able to express it interestingly. Such people may only need a few pointers before giving their first public talks. Many good books on public speaking are available at your library.

The greatest benefit you and your co-advocates gain from public exposure is that you personally acquaint influential people with the needs of the retired. And you will be able to call on them for assistance later, just as I have done countless times when support or money was needed to help the retired in my own community.

SENIOR ACTIVISM

The retired are their own best promoters.

If I could suggest an active retirement pursuit for retired people, it would be the one I've chosen for myself—involvement in the community affairs of the retired. I am as busy now as I was when I was a working engineer. And the work I am doing is as important for the people I deal with and for future generations of the retired as my inventions were for industry in previous years.

Advocacy should be the business of the retired, for they have the time, energy, and life experiences to make it successful. If you are looking for a full-time retirement pursuit to keep you feeling young and vigorous and in the mainstream of American life, retirement activism just may be it. The gratifications are immeasurable.

9 A MODEL OF WHAT CAN BE ACCOMPLISHED: Ventura County, California

The keys to success are: organize, plan, and persevere.

Let me give you an idea of what you can accomplish for the seniors in your area by describing some of the programs we've developed in Ventura County in a period of five years. Some of them require nothing more than the cooperation of local government agencies and the generosity of interested citizens. Others, such as the Skill Bank, require little more than some cards, a shoe box to keep them in, and organization and time. Still others involve the participation of, and funding by, the federal government.

GETTING WHAT YOU WANT WITHOUT FEDERAL MONEY

Our senior center.

I know the great value of going down to a senior center, meeting my peers, and recruiting their assistance. But if there is no senior center in your community, as was the case when I first arrived in Thousand Oaks, what do you do? You begin advocating for one.

Ours became quite an extraordinary event. We seized upon a chance opportunity, involved as many retired as we could, and successfully achieved our purpose. Your story will certainly be different, but the same premise underlies all the accomplishments of the retired in Ventura County and in any other community: nothing is achieved easily, nothing is handed out. Everything that is accomplished comes after a relentless struggle. Organization, planning, and above all, perseverance are responsible for success.

We began our campaign for a senior center by hounding our city council. After repeated trips to city hall, the city finally agreed to a temporary compromise solution and rented a social club for us for weekdays. The trouble was they also rented it out in the evening for big parties and when we would arrive next day the place would be a shambles. It always took several hours to clean up before we could even tolerate staying inside. Still, it was better than nothing. But we didn't stop our efforts. We continued to press city officials for our own permanent senior center. Soon our advocacy, in the form of letters, phone calls, petitions, and meetings generated a lot of publicity in the news media.

Then our first big break came. A large, modern one-story building used as a sales promotion office by land developers had been singled out for demolition. The building was only three years old, but the land on which it stood had been sold to make way for a high-rise office building. The architect in charge of the project decided tearing it down was the most economical way to remove it. However, he had heard about our clamoring for a senior center, and decided to call to see if we could use the building. We said of course we could, even though nobody had a clue about what was actually involved.

We soon found out. The first thing we learned was that the building had to be moved off the property in thirty days or it would be demolished. Then we learned there was no understructure covering the slab foundation, so no conventional way could be used to transfer it. We also had no place to move it to, since the city's recreation and parks district had already told us it could not give us any land on which to locate our senior center.

We began formulating tactics. First, we established a senior center advisory committee of thirty people to handle the various problems. Then we began generating as much publicity as we could, because we had no funds at all, and we knew we were going to need a lot of help.

Then the second break came. A man who owned an industrial moving business read of our problems and offered to move the building free. He said the only way to do it was to put steel beams through the roof and let the building hang from its roof beams. Its concrete floor would be left behind.

Terrific. We had the mover and the building but still no place to move it to. We turned to the city's recreation and parks district again. We were turned down. We even went to a large supermarket and asked if we could place the building on the back part of their parking lot until such time as land became available. They said no.

Nothing was as unexpected, though, as what finally happened. Our third break came when Louis Goebel, a senior who had made money building Jungle Land, a reserve for wild animals used in the movies, took this moment to generously donate an acre of prime land, worth about $50,000, that had its own capped artesian well.

Still, we couldn't just set the building on the ground without a floor. There had to be a foundation, and we still had no money. Then our fourth big break came. Frank Lussier, a young architect, heard of our difficulties and volunteered to lay the plans out for the ground floor free. He donated what amounted to thousands of dollars of his time until the city finally approved his architectural plan.

Now we had the plans but still lacked money with which to build the foundation. We went back to the city and found the officials more receptive now, because (a) we had a $50,000 parcel of land and (b) a modern building worth an estimated hundred thousand dollars. So things began falling into place, and we drew up the following agreement: the city would take possession of the building as public property, and the recreation and parks district would supply a staff to run and maintain it. On that basis, the city agreed to pay for the foundation.

But our troubles weren't quite over yet. Every step of the way, other matters continued to threaten the project. Once the building was set on its foundation, the city said we had to tear off the wooden roof and put on a tile roof to ensure fire safety. The tile would cost $7,000. Again, there was no money available. Back we went to the public for help through the news media. One morning a huge pile of red adobe tile shingles was found stacked outside our building. The donor, a contractor who was constructing homes in Thousand Oaks, left a note wishing us good luck.

Now we needed roofers. Again our appeal went out through local television and newspapers. It brought out enough volunteers to put the entire roof up in a single weekend.

Now that all the major problems had been licked, retired people began bringing tools out of their garages to put on the finishing touches. They painted walls, scraped and tiled floors, put in new windows, relaid the rugs, and put in landscaping using plants from the old building site.

It was an amazing effort by a determined group of people. I estimate that nearly a thousand retired persons played a decisive role in accomplishing the project. Some were even hurt in the process—one old-timer broke his foot, many cut their hands and arms. But I never heard anyone complain.

Now each day 300 retired people use the center they made for themselves. It has a large lounge with a fireplace, a meeting room that can accommodate 300, a library, a room with a pool table, a sewing room, kitchen, crafts/machine shop, and three offices. And the whole place is air-condi-

tioned by the system that was installed in the original
building. We couldn't ask for anything more. But it didn't
happen by itself.

SENIOR SURVIVAL COURSES

In the spring of 1973 I realized that there were a great
many people needing to know the facts of economic survival who weren't being reached. There were too many nonretired who had no satisfactory plans for their future and
too many retired who were getting far less income or
medical care than they were entitled to. So I developed the
idea of a course in senior survival.

I went to the community colleges in the county with a
proposal to sponsor such a course. None would do it. They
said seniors wouldn't be interested in going to school again.
I began a campaign to bring them around to my point of
view. I went to the meetings of the college trustees and
cornered administrators wherever I could. I pointed out
their obligation to 44,000 retired citizens in the county, and
the fact that 60 percent of their property taxes went toward
public education—from which they received no value at all
in return.

Finally, after a year one of the community colleges
agreed to start a class. But then they couldn't find anyone
to teach it or any satisfactory textbook on the subject, and
were going to cancel the class before it even got started. I
couldn't let that happen, so I told them I would do the
teaching and would provide the text. I needed accreditation
to teach and spent a week filling out forms to prove, among
other things, that I was a college graduate and that I didn't
have tuberculosis. The state finally accredited me, and the
first classes were announced.

Of course there were problems right away. There always
are. The college had publicized the class, by mistake, for
two different locations at the same time. I asked my daugh-

ter, Irene Brown, who is knowledgeable in retired people's affairs, to teach one class, I would teach the other. Seven showed up for Irene's class, six for mine. It was exactly what the college had feared—no interest among the retired for such a class—and once again they wanted to drop it from the curriculum.

I persuaded them to let me handle the arrangements for the next session, assured them it would be a success, and asked for a free hand. They agreed. The first thing I did was to get publicity out to the newspapers and radio, something the college had not done. Then I changed the location of the class to a building in the heart of an area where seniors lived.

That got results. Not six or seven but 130 students showed up. For the six weeks' duration of the course, attendance averaged eighty-two retired people, which delighted the college because they received $3 in state money for every student they enrolled. Then when word of its success spread, the original college and several others in the county were flooded with requests from residents in four of the neighboring cities to begin similar classes. I couldn't teach them all, so I trained tutors. To date, I've graduated 112 tutors.

I never did find any usable textbooks, though. Most of the ones I read seemed to be written by younger people who had no idea about the special problems seniors face. And most of these books, I'm sure without any harmful intent, perpetuate the Great Retirement Lie. So with my input and funds provided by the college, my daughter wrote the texts.

SENIOR ADVOCACY COURSES

It was only logical that my next senior course would deal with senior advocacy. It's not enough for retired people to know how to survive with what society has

left them. They must also know how to change society for
their benefit.

This time when I approached college administrators to
sponsor a class they went for the idea. The survival classes,
after all, had such drawing power that they often had to be
held in the college cafeteria. I wanted the new class to be
called "How to Fight City Hall and Win." The college
insisted on a less-threatening name, and we settled on "Senior Advocacy."

The first class, held in October 1975, has been followed
by a stream of others and have graduated several hundred
better prepared advocates. Much of what I've taught them is
contained in the previous chapter of this book. I've also
enlisted the help of guest speakers—mayors of various cities
in my county, congressional representatives, and federal
officials. This way would-be advocates see and hear first-
hand people at various government levels whom they will be
meeting later. The officials and politicians, by the way,
enjoy coming as guests, since they have begun to realize the
political power of retired people. Needless to say,
appearances at such community projects are good publicity
in the nonsenior community, too. The news media have also
taken to the classes, and reporters often sit in, especially
when public figures are guest lecturers. Several classes have
been televised. One class has been developed that will be
broadcast regularly on radio.

NEWSLETTERS

A good way to keep seniors informed is by sending out a
newsletter. In it you can put all the information that retired
people should get that can't or won't fit into the newspaper.
(Besides, some retirees don't read the paper every day.)

We've started two in my own area. My daughter, Irene
Lamb Brown, is the editor of both. One is paid for by the

college where I teach my senior advocacy course. The other is financed by a grant from a charitable organization, and the postage is paid by the local public school district.

The funding to start the newsletters was obtained after forceful presentations to several groups who had money for such enterprises. We didn't simply go in and demand the money. We prepared our case well, spoke firmly but politely, and demonstrated the need for the retired to be better informed. The result was that we got exactly what we wanted and needed.

Now some 6,500 newsletters are mailed out each month and read by an estimated 13,000 retired persons. The newsletter includes any information that could help a senior, from tips on how to solve a Social Security problem to a listing of locations where seniors can get free flu shots. If a law that affects a senior changes, the newsletter explains it clearly. If a radio program of interest is aired, time and station are provided.

THE SKILL BANK

The more familiar I became with the retired citizens of Ventura County, the more I recognized how much time, energy, and money we could all save by helping each other, simply by trading our skills. People are resources, and in skilled people we were rich. So the Skill Bank began as a common-sense way to use the neglected talents of retired people.

I started to keep track of the skills of seniors I met. I found master plumbers, accountants, tax lawyers, seamstresses, carpenters—a whole range of skills, crafts, and professions. One of the earliest opportunities I had to match skill with need was when I met a retired woman whose old vacuum cleaner had broken down. When she had taken it to a dealer, the serviceman told her the machine was at least thirty years old, and since they no longer even made parts for it he wouldn't look at it. But what do you do when you don't have money to buy a new one?

As it happened, I knew a senior who boasted there was nothing in the world he couldn't fix, all he needed was a hairpin and chewing gum. So I took the vacuum cleaner to him. He took it apart and found that all that was wrong was that some fibers from a shag rug had caught around the rubber pulley that turned the brushes. He cleaned it out, oiled, and adjusted it, and it ran like new.

The lady was so delighted with the results, she asked if she could do something for him in return. He said the tops of his windows hadn't been washed in four or five years because he had arthritis in his arms, so she went over one day and cleaned the windows and washed the curtains.

After that I started compiling index cards of all the skilled retired people I met and asked them if they would mind lending their talents and a little time to other retired persons if the occasion arose. All said they would. Most of the skilled craftsmen still had all their tools. Later I set up tables on the sidewalk in front of a clinic when the state started giving free flu shots to seniors, and I and other volunteers asked seniors who were leaving if they would mind giving us the information we needed to start our Skill Bank, and in return we would send them literature on senior affairs that could benefit them and also help them research their Social Security benefits.

After that sign-up at the clinic word spread quickly and pretty soon we had more than 5,000 names and skills to swap.

APPLYING FOR
GOVERNMENT FUNDING

The money is there.

Whether you want to start a hot meals or senior bus program, or free clinic, most of the money to launch these programs must come from the federal government. And the number of grants available is amazing.

Learning about federal grants is probably best accomplished by acquainting yourself with people who keep tabs on such things. City and county administrators, planners, and the like may have valuable information. A letter to the local office of your congressional representative could tip you off to federal money that is available. Legislators and representatives are good sources of information. Also, for a full list of federal grants available, check your library for a copy of *The Catalog of Federal Domestic Assistance.*

Although citizens' groups may apply for grants, you're better off going through the local governing body, which already is recognized as a responsible grant recipient. However, many community administrators are ignorant about these grants or lazy about applying, so the senior advocate may have to do the groundwork.

First, you have to research the various grants and see if the stipulations can be met. For instance, your community may be requested to put up funds amounting to 10 or 20 percent of the total federal grant. In addition, it must be proved that your area needs the grant more than another area, and that it will actually improve the lives of the retired people in your community. The plain fact is that the grants go to the groups that apply for them and who make the strongest cases for their need. That's why it helps to have an organized group of advocates and supporters behind you. With a lot of people looking for ways to get available money and ways to build your argument, the task becomes easier.

Then all that information needs to be brought to the attention of the city council, board of supervisors, or other local governing body so that it can do the applying for you.

Many of our programs had to be funded with federal money, and once we had determined what the priorities were for our community, we applied for many of the grants at the same time. This is a good idea because some of the applications will be turned down, and if you scatter your

shots you are bound to have some success. Most of the
money for our projects came from federal money
granted under the Older Americans Act. We applied for
it through our state's Office on Aging, which (as is true
in most states) is the official agency that disburses federal money for senior needs. (In Appendix E I've listed
all the addresses of the state Offices on Aging.) A
smaller percentage of our money came from philan-
thropic organizations, a listing of which can be found at
the library in the *Annual Register of Grant Support* or
the *Foundation of Grants Index.*

Before we go any further in our discussion of how to get
and use community, state, and federal money, let me make
one statement that is an absolute rule for anyone who
wishes to maintain credibility and durability. Always keep
careful records of all grant money you receive; let the
disbursing agency know how carefully you spent it, and
spare no words about how efficient and successful the
programs operated by it are.

The battle to get federal funds is fought on two fronts.
First, you have to convince the state office that disburses
the federal funds to release the money for your project.
Second, you have to convince your local government to put
up its share of qualifying funds.

As I've said earlier, a sound argument to use with local
governments is that any federal money that comes into the
local community—whether earmarked for senior services or
in the form of Social Security checks—is money-in-action
that enriches the local economy. It multiplies four times
before it leaves. Any statistician can verify that economic
fact.

Before I came, Ventura County was receiving no federal
money at all for senior programs. A year after I arrived, it
was receiving $75,000 a year. Currently, it is getting nearly
$400,000 a year. Roughly four times that amount—$1.6
million in total purchases—is now being injected into the
local economy.

HOT MEALS DINING SITES

Today about 400 retired people in Ventura County can come to one of eleven designated dining sites at noontime for a hot nourishing meal. Although a donation of fifty cents is suggested, the meal is free to seniors who cannot afford to pay. There is no third degree if a senior doesn't. He or she is entitled to that lunch.

It began in 1974 when the first "hot meals" program in the county was instituted through funds contributed from a Title VII grant from the federal government under the Older Americans Act. Initially, application for the grant had to be made through the state Office on Aging in Sacramento. At first, they told me there was just no chance, that federal money for senior dining sites was going into big-city ghettos. I told them that many of our seniors were just as hungry as the people in the city and argued that the money should be disbursed on a percentage-of-population basis. I told some of the stories of hardship I've already told you about retired people in the county. I investigated how dining sites were operated in other areas like Los Angeles, and went back to Sacramento with specific proposals of how we would operate our own dining site.

The officials in the Office on Aging were impressed but held back. They said they would look more favorably on the request if Ventura County practiced what it preached; that is, if the county did something on its own first before seeking federal aid.

I decided to try to get a school to do the demonstration. The principals of the first two schools I approached turned me down, but the third agreed to feed ten needy retired grandmothers one meal a day for fifty days. Local donations covered the costs. I dutifully reported that to Sacramento and continued to send in other personal stories of hardship. I followed the strategy described in the last chapter and talked personally to each administrator in the Office on Aging. I was always courteous and businesslike no matter how frustrated I felt at continually being turned down. Finally, it happened. They agreed to finance a pilot project, seventy-five people a day. That battle had taken six months.

Since that first federally funded dining site, we have shown that our county could run such a program efficiently and that there is a continuing need. Now we have eleven dining sites and enough money to feed 400 people one good hot meal a day.

THE NUTRITIONMOBILE AND
MEALS ON WHEELS

Once we had the hot meals dining site program under way, I wanted to tackle the problem of the needy retired who couldn't get to the sites. Some of the poorest of the retired lived on the outskirts of the cities. One ninety-three-year-old man had lost his driver's license years before because the state felt he was too old to drive. Even so, he still had to drive into town (at night, to avoid the sheriff) once a week to buy food.

I went back to the Office on Aging and applied for some more money under the Older Americans Act. My idea was to have a "Nutritionmobile," a truck with a driver to shop for these retired people. They would make out a shopping list and pay for the food, just as if they had gone to the store themselves, but they wouldn't pay as much because prices in the city supermarkets would be lower than those in the local country stores. The truck could also pick up prescriptions and other such items. In addition, I felt the truck should have cooking facilities so hot meals could be provided to those too ill to cook for themselves.

When I took my proposal to the Office on Aging, they thought it was ridiculous. When I pointed out that we had been successful on the hot meals dining site program, they agreed to give us enough money to operate a Nutritionmobile as a "model research project." To comply with federal regulations, however, the county had to put up 20 percent of the $40,000 the federal government was chipping in. I showed county officials that their $8,000 share could come in the form of supplies and office space to operate the project, and they agreed.

Now we have our Nutritionmobile going around to the outlying areas providing services to more than 400 needy seniors. It is driven by a social worker who knows the people he serves on a first-name basis. When he drives up to their homes, he blows a special horn on the truck so they know he's there. If one of his regulars does not come out of the house, he checks to see that everything is all right. If he finds someone is ill, he gets a public health nurse out. If he discovers a yard gate broken or a toilet clogged, he arranges for a volunteer to fix it.

The Nutritionmobile was only one way we got food to people who couldn't get it for themselves. The federal government said we could use up to 10 percent of the money for the hot meals dining sites to deliver meals to the homes of retired people, so we created a Meals on Wheels program. This program recruited volunteers to deliver hot meals to seniors unable to reach the fixed dining sites, and it has been highly successful and satisfying, both to the volunteers assisting and to the seniors it assists.

SENIOR SURVIVAL SERVICES

When you work among retired people it doesn't take long to realize that some are caught in a crunch on the weekend and on holidays because everything is closed. Another bad time is the end of the month when their Social Security money runs out. In every community in this country there are thousands of retired people who dread the approach of the end of the month because it means a time of deprivation until their next check arrives. They run out of food; their electricity or gas is shut off because they are late with the payments; they run out of medicine. The discomforts and deprivations are countless.

I realized we needed twenty-four hour, seven-day-a-week service so these people could get emergency help. What I had in mind was the creation of a system by which a senior in need could call a toll-free county number at any hour to reach a trained worker ready to assist. Once again I went to the Sacramento Office on Aging to request funds for such a service. Once again I was turned down. Next I approached the county board of supervisors to ask them to start a small "senior survival services" program, hoping the state might start a broader program later after they saw how well it worked. I knew, however, this would be a hard program to sell the supervisors, so I tried a slightly different strategy than I'd used in Sacramento. I took advantage of a local controversy involving stray dogs.

Everybody in the county seemed to be after the board of supervisors to do something about the "dog problem." It seemed that when animal control officers went home at night, they kept a pocket beeper with them so that if a dog was in trouble an officer could be summoned to rescue it. In other words, there were funds available to help a dog in an emergency but none to provide help for a senior who might be starving over a weekend.

I invited the supervisors to a committee meeting at the local senior center. On the blackboard I had written in big letters, *DOGS ARE TREATED BETTER THAN SENIORS IN VENTURA COUNTY*. After the meeting the supervisors asked me what it would cost to treat seniors as well as dogs. Off the top of my head I said $5,000. I figured you could start some kind of a program with that amount, and it was modest enough for them to at least consider. The supervisors gave the matter to their staff to study. The staff came back and said $5,000 just wouldn't be enough and the county couldn't afford more. They turned me down.

I was not deterred—as no advocate must be. I went back to Sacramento. I suggested that they fund the program as another "model research project." They said no. I came back with one more alternative. I said we would scrap the whole idea if it didn't work out after a couple of months' trial. That's what did it, and this is where persistence paid off. Or maybe they did it just to get me off their back.

The senior survival services program has since been renewed and is now in its third year. It is funded by the federal government, under Title III of the Older Americans Act, which gives the county $66,000 a year to run it. The county's share is about $13,000. At present, the program has two survival workers who are available around the clock to respond to any emergency. The workers even have beepers—just like the dog catchers.

THE SURVIVALMOBILE FLEET

Sometimes you discover there just doesn't seem to be any money available at all for some programs. Such was the case with my idea for a Survivalmobile fleet. I envisioned it as a group of drivers with cars and vans who would be available around the clock to take seniors somewhere in an emergency or to places they couldn't get to by bus. They could also deliver groceries to people not served by the Nutritionmobile. For a variety of reasons, seniors need transportation to keep living healthy, relatively comfortable lives. I felt the Survivalmobile fleet would be a good answer.

But the seniors and I were the only ones who felt that way. When I went before the Ventura County Association of Governments to ask them for money, one member walked out, saying he'd have nothing to do with giving anyone a free ride. One city manager called my idea "a glorified taxi service from one end of the county to the other." And everybody else turned me down for funds, all the way from county to state. But I had an ace up my sleeve, as every advocate will find he or she has, after thinking about a problem long enough.

At the same time I was looking for money to start the Survivalmobile fleet, I was preparing my monthly report on all the programs for the state Office on Aging. I had always kept careful records of any money received to run these programs. I never spent a dime more than needed, because if I could show how efficient my programs were, I realized it would increase my chances of getting more money later. My reports showed that I had held the line so well on the senior survival services program that I had several thousand dollars left over. Rather than return the money I persuaded the state Office on Aging to let me use it to try my Survivalmobile idea. By then, I had such a good track record for spending money carefully and effectively that they gave me the go-ahead.

With the seed money, I went to work. I recruited forty drivers from the retired community on a stand-by plan, paying $2.30 an hour, plus fourteen cents a mile. It wasn't much money, but it had a double-barreled impact: it offered an invaluable service to the retired and at the same time gave a part-time job to other retirees.

It worked. The Survivalmobile fleet is still in its first year but has received write-ups in several national magazines as a creative service to seniors. Hopefully, it will prepare the way for other communities to follow our lead.

BUS TRANSPORTATION

Not only is money sometimes hard to get, but often services are, too. You have to continually grind away at the obstacles, think of all possible solutions, and wear the opposition down until you achieve your goal.

Bus transportation, probably one of the most crucial needs of the retired, is one of these hard-to-get things. This is true in most places, the reason being that it involves a high financial commitment on the part of the community.

When I first came to Ventura County, only Greyhound connected its nine cities. And, except for two cities, there was no bus service within the cities. Now, as a result of pressure from many retired people, seven bus systems serve the cities and connect them to each other. In several areas, the retired advocates even persuaded the local governments to provide free bus service for seniors.

The biggest and most progressive bus system in the county is called SCAT (South Coast Area Transit). That system, I realized, was where we had to make inroads. At the time, it cost seventy-five cents to ride from Ojai to Port Hueneme, a distance of twenty-five miles. That was a $1.50 round trip, but some retired people just couldn't afford that much money. It took a year of fighting—I must have argued before the SCAT board twenty times—to reduce the fare for retired people to fifteen cents. Finally we got it down to a dime.

The day they decided to drop the fare to ten cents, I asked them also to consider giving the very oldest seniors free rides. I don't think they quite believed I had the audacity to ask for this after they had just agreed to the reduced fares. It was impossible, they said, because seniors comprise 25 percent of the riders, and it would mean too great a loss of revenue. I protested that the retired had been paying all their lives, and that it was time the oldest of them got to ride free.

They asked me what age I thought the retired should be to ride free. "Everyone over 100." I said. They looked astonished.

"How many free riders would that make?"

"Probably about ten," I said.

"Well," they said, "maybe the age limit could be a little bit lower."

I suggested that the SCAT board pick an age they thought they could live with. If I could get them to give free rides to one age group, the start would have been made and we could work the age limit down over the years.

Months went by before I heard anything more. Eventually, they told me it would cost a quarter of a million dollars to provide free rides to older retired persons. And no wonder. The age limit they had picked was sixty. Of course that wouldn't work, I answered. That's why I had suggested 100. Finally, we compromised. The SCAT board agreed to allow seniors over the age of seventy-four to ride free if their incomes were below $4,000 a year. That agreement climaxed twelve months of haggling. The newspapers played it up big, and the SCAT board got a lot of praise for its wisdom and generosity.

In two years only 500 retired people have received free bus-ride cards. Hardly a costly matter. It seems to me the door is wide open to ask the SCAT board to drop the income restriction and lower the age limit to seventy. Eventually perhaps we can get them to lower it to sixty-five. But those things take time, and time is what the advocate must be willing to give to the cause.

A FEW OTHER ACHIEVEMENTS

What else can be accomplished with senior advocacy.

Let me just list briefly a few other benefits the retired have gained in Ventura County as a result of their advocacy. Perhaps it will give you some hope, ideas, and direction for your own community.

The Homemaking Service provides free homemaking care to the retired recovering from illnesses.

Senior Discounts furnish people over sixty with discounts of from 10 to 50 percent at some 400 participating stores.

Utility Rate Reductions are available in some cities for persons, old or young, who use very little of the utility. In Thousand Oaks a retired person can get as much as a 96 percent reduction on sewer and water rates.

Retired Senior Volunteer Programs have existed in some cities for years in which retired people are recruited to perform volunteer services for other needy retireds.

The Foster Grandparents Program links hundreds of retired people with children for the purpose of companionship for both groups.

Tel Med Tapes is a series of three- to five-minute tape recordings about health that a person may listen to by dialing a toll-free number.

Survival Gardens are among our works-in-progress. As you can see, no new idea takes hold right away. At one time I proposed that some of the 1,566 acres of unused, undeveloped park land in Ventura County be turned into "survival gardens" for retired people. My idea was to give seniors exercise as well as a way to stretch food budgets by growing their own fruits and vegetables. It would cost the county nothing, but we needed permission to till the land.

A few survival gardens started here and there, but not on any significant scale. The officials dragged their feet until the idea lost public support. But we haven't given up. We've just been busy getting other projects under way. Someday we'll have those survival gardens on the unused land, and then "the desert will bloom."

THE THEORY BEHIND ADVOCACY

Hammering away with better tactics until you achieve your goal.

I've talked a bit about the theory behind advocacy. Now that you've read some of the programs that have been successful in my area, perhaps you can see the general pattern used to achieve that success. First, we *organized*, then *planned* our goals well, and *persevered* while trying to achieve them. Second, we were willing to compromise when necessary. You can't get everything at once, but once you have your foot in the door you're almost home. Third, where our own efforts proved inadequate, we went to the public for support. Not all of our efforts bore fruit immediately, of course, but we never gave up.

Finally, we were willing to change course when it became clear that our tactics were ineffective. I'm an old inventor, and an inventor, to be successful, realizes very quickly that you first try for the orthodox solution; if that doesn't work, go for the unorthodox, the new, the novel way. When I suggest that the advocate persevere in pursuing a goal, I don't mean hammering away with the same old tactic day after day. I mean hammering away day after day with newer and better strategy and ideas—until you achieve your goal.

In my opinion, Ventura County is now the most progressive area in California in responding to the needs of its retired population. (California is easily the most progressive state in the country.) The programs we have are the most innovative and comprehensive anywhere, and the public officials charged with dealing with the retired have become very cooperative in searching for solutions to the problems of the retired. What we have done can be done elsewhere.

10 A GLIMPSE INTO A BETTER FUTURE

The ends are clear. The means are participation by all people—now.

The programs I have discussed up until now, even those requiring the use of federal money, have been directed at improving retirement in local communities, and it is on that level that you can be most effective. However, it is obvious we need a sensible national policy toward retirement. We need to make life for older people more productive and worthwhile. Various forward-looking people thinking about these problems have suggested the following twelve goals.

End Mandatory Retirement

Everyone should be allowed to work as long as he or she can perform the job. Turning sixty-five should not be the criterion that determines when a person is terminated.

For those of us who are employed by others, forced retirement is unavoidable. Approximately 50 percent of all working Americans are employed by companies that have compulsory retirement policies. The other 50 percent are subjected to other pressures to retire: attacks on work performance, hints that they are no longer needed, and so on.

It wasn't always this way. Forced retirement initially grew out of a humanitarian idea. During the Great Depression, legislation was enacted to provide Social Security for retired workers over sixty-five in order to give them incentive to quit and make room in the job market for younger workers who had families to feed. Today, however, mandatory retirement at age sixty-five has become routine practice in business and government.

But mandatory retirement of older workers is no longer beneficial- to the economy. In fact, it is harmful. Older workers are often retired at the peak of their productive powers. They have spent a lifetime developing and refining the skills that their replacements have only begun to learn. This is a tremendous loss to a company. Older workers also have the benefit of experience and maturity, which sharpen their judgment. Finally, retirement deprives the country of the income taxes such workers would have paid, and instead adds more demands to the already overstrained Social Security system.

As I mentioned before, in 1900 people over sixty-five made up 36 percent of the labor force. Today, only 14 percent. And a 1974 Harris poll showed that nearly 40 percent would still prefer to be working.

Other countries have a different philosophy about their older workers and, as a result, different policies. Because some are experiencing a severe labor shortage, they entice their older workers to keep working. Sweden, for instance, has raised its retirement age level to sixty-seven and provides incentives to delay retirement. In the United States, by contrast, the retirement age is going down, not up. Even people as young as forty-five are being caught in the snare. In 1965, before there was much thought about discrimination because of age, the U.S. Labor Department reported that in the twenty states with no age discrimination laws, 25 percent of the available job openings were closed to applicants over forty-five, and nearly all were closed to applicants over fifty-five. Mandatory retirement doesn't just affect those in their sixties.

Guarantee Pension Plans

Ralph Nader and Kate Blackwell wrote a book in 1973 called *You and Your Pension.* In it they pointed out the flaws of private pension plans in the United States. It's one book all legislators should read before drafting the next pension reform bill, because millions of retired people are still being cheated out of their pensions each year. By the time they learn of the theft, however, they are too old to renew their careers again and opt for a sounder plan. The next pension reform bill must remedy this situation.

Increase Social Security Benefits

The Social Security system may well be in trouble. But somehow payments must be increased to guarantee a better than subsistence-level income for the retired.

Establish National Health Insurance

Medicare is ineffective and should be exchanged for a national health insurance plan for all Americans. Medical care in this country is not only costly for the retired, it's costly for the young as well. In addition, tighter regulation of health-care insurance companies is urgently needed to prevent the automatic exclusion of retired people from adequate insurance programs. Insurance companies should also be prevented from offering industries a reduced insur-

ance premium for not employing older workers. This is an
effective inducement to employers to adopt or continue the
policy of mandatory retirement. Exactly what we don't
need.

Have Government-Paid Medications

The government should aid the retired by paying for
out-of-hospital prescription drugs not covered by Medicare.
Although the elderly make up 11 percent of the population,
they use and pay for 25 percent of all prescribed drugs, and
they are often the ones who can *least* afford it.

Teach More Gerontological Medicine

Doctors are often ignorant of the ills of older patients
and callous toward sick seniors. Therefore, medical schools
should include gerontological studies as a regular part of
their curriculum.

Regulate Nursing Homes

Closer supervision of nursing homes is needed to ensure
that the institutionalized retired are cared for, not simply
stored away. The government should play a greater role in
caring for the elderly in nursing homes by granting subsidies
to qualified homes. It should also play a greater role in
rating the nursing home industry in order to weed out those
who prey on the elderly.

Institute Special Transportation

Inexpensive transportation is one of the essential needs of
the elderly. Without it many are homebound and unable to

use community resources. The best way to meet this problem is through mass transit, which also benefits the young, or through special bus transportation for seniors no longer able to drive.

Control Rents

Every state should pass rent control laws to prevent landlords from arbitrarily increasing rents to evict the retired, who are sometimes regarded as undesirable tenants.

Reduce Property Taxes

Property taxes should be frozen or reduced once a person is retired in order to prevent retirees with fixed incomes from being forced out of their homes because of inability to pay soaring taxes.

Reduce Utility Rates

All persons should pay only for the utility services they actually use, which is often one-fourth what others (say, a family of four) use.

Establish Senior Foundations

Nonprofit senior foundations, operated by seniors themselves, should be established nationally to respond to emergency problems of the retired.

There are a lot of other changes needed. Interest from savings up to a certain amount for the retired should not be taxed. The amount of money that one can earn and still keep Social Security payments should be increased. The loss of benefits upon remarriage should be cut out entirely.

GOVERNMENT AND THE RETIRED

*Does anyone care? It's your job to
make them.*

At present, the attitude of the federal, state, and local governments roughly parallels that of the medical profession in its ignorance and indifference toward the problems of the retired.

What is needed is a strong department of senior affairs at the cabinet level, staffed by retired people who have first-hand, expert knowledge of the problems of their peers. And the department should have sufficient power to respond effectively to the problems that come its way.

Politicians worry about the "economic feasibility" of new programs—of increasing Social Security payments, of improving the medical delivery system to the retired, and of accomplishing the other retirement goals I outlined in this book. But economic feasibility ultimately depends not only on the wealth of a nation, but also its values and regard for the quality of human life. Other countries—most, in fact—give a greater proportion of their wealth to the retired than the United States does. While the United States grosses nearly a trillion dollars a year, it spends only about 4.2 percent toward helping older Americans. France and Britain, though less affluent, each spend close to 7 percent of their Gross National Product to help their older citizens. Our country should have just as strong a sense of moral responsibility.

YOU ARE AT THE CONTROLS

Getting the golden years you deserve.

The question to those already retired is, do you think you are getting what you deserve after working forty or fifty years? And to those of you who are not yet retired, will you permit yourself to slip into retirement before you realize that the "golden years" you were promised are not going to happen after all? You can change retirement from a threat to a reward. I've told you how to go about it. Now it's up to you.

If you have any questions or problems with which you think I might be able to help you, I would be happy to offer my services. Send a stamped, self-addressed envelope to P.O. Box 532, Newbury Park, California 91320.—*Tony Lamb*

RECOMMENDED READING

Arthur, Julietta K., *Retire to Action*. Nashville and New York: Abingdon Press, 1969. Excellent, well-organized book for retired persons who want to volunteer to help others.

Brown, Irene Lamb, *"Tony Lamb's Senior Survival Basics."* Newbury Park, Calif.: Richard Lamb, 1977. Collection of teaching manuals used by Tony Lamb in his senior survival and advocacy courses.

Butler, Robert N., *Why Survive? Being Old in America*. New York: Harper & Row, 1975. Definitive exploration and documentation on the problems of the elderly and recommendations for alleviating them.

Cooley, Leland F., and Lee M. Cooley, *How to Avoid the Retirement Trap*. Los Angeles: Nash, 1972. Dramatic, honest retirement planner.

Curtin, Sharon R., *Nobody Ever Died of Old Age*. Boston: Atlantic Monthly Press, 1973. Beautifully written account of the hardships of being old in America.

David, William, *Not Quite Ready to Retire*. New York: Collier Books, 1970. Valuable reference guide to jobs for the retired.

Denenberg, Herbert S., *Getting Your Money's Worth*. Washington, D.C.: Public Affairs Press, 1974. Excellent guide to buying insurance of all types.

Hardy, C. Colburn, *Funk and Wagnalls Guide to Personal Money Management*. New York: Funk and Wagnalls, 1976. Excellent lay guide to shrewd money management.

Olmstead, Alan H., *Threshold: The First Days of Retirement*. New York: Harper & Row, 1975. One man's personal diary of the first year of retirement.

Shore, Warren, *Social Security: The Fraud in Your Future*. New York: Macmillan. 1975. Investigative report on the insecurity of Social Security.

APPENDIX A
Government Volunteer and Employment Programs for Retired People

The following volunteer and employment programs open to senior citizens are sponsored by ACTION, Washington, D.C. 20525:

Peace Corps. Volunteers teach needed skills to the poor of other countries. There is no upper age limit.

Retired Senior Volunteer Program (RSVP). Funds volunteer programs to aid public and nonprofit institutions; volunteers paid travel and meal expenses.

Service Corps of Retired Executives (SCORE). Administered by the Small Business Administration to help new businesses by providing them with experienced advisors.

Volunteers in Service to America (VISTA). Helps impoverished Americans in urban and rural areas. Volunteers receive living expenses, medical care, and a small salary. There is no upper age limit.

Three other government volunteer and employment programs are:

International Executive Service Corps (IESC)
545 Madison Ave.
New York, N.Y. 10022
Sponsors aid to overseas countries by American executives, supported in part by government funding.

International Voluntary Services, Inc. (IVS)
1555 Connecticut Ave., N.W.
Washington, D.C. 20036
Government agencies provide more than half of the funding for this private organization, which sponsors well-educated volunteers in science, medicine, social work, and education. Most assignments last at least two years and are in Asia, Africa, and Latin America. Daily expenses and a salary are paid.

National Center for Voluntary Action (NCVA)
1625 Massachusetts Ave., N.W.
Washington, D.C. 20336
Serves as a volunteer-project clearinghouse. Its main function is to collect information on projects, gather technical expertise in volunteer areas, and give advice on how to organize volunteer service projects. If you want to organize a project, write and ask for material in your field of interest.

Persons over sixty with low incomes—below Office of Economic Opportunity (OEO) guidelines—are eligible for the following employment programs:

APPENDIX B
Other Employment for Retired People

Foster Grandparents, sponsored by ACTION, Washington, D.C. 20525. Gives friendship and care to institutionalized orphans and mentally retarded children for twenty hours per week at minimum wages.

Green Thumb (men) and *Green Light* (women), sponsored by the National Farmers Union, Green Thumb/Green Light, 1012 14th St., N.W., Washington, D.C. Provide conservation and landscaping and community services.

Operation Mainstream programs, funded by the Department of Labor to help chronically unemployed poor, especially those over forty.

Senior Aides, sponsored by the National Council of Senior Citizens, 1511 K St., N.W., Washington, D.C. 20005. Provides community services.

Senior Community Service programs, sponsored by the National Council on the Aging, 1828 L St., N.W., Washington, D.C. 20036.

Senior Community Service Aides, sponsored by the National Retired Teachers Association, Senior Community Service Aides Project, 1225 Connecticut Ave., N.W., Washington, D.C. 20036.

Senior Opportunities for Service (SOS) programs, sponsored by the Office of Economic Opportunity, Office of Program Review, Washington, D.C. 20506. Provides services in nutrition, consumer education, and outreach services for older people.

The following organizations offer employment counseling, testing, and placement services for the older worker:

American Association on Emeriti
1036 Tiverton Ave., Suite 5
Los Angeles, Calif. 90024
For retired or retiring academic personnel. Publishes listing.

Catholic Vocation Service of the Archdiocese of N.Y.
122 E. 22nd St.
New York, N.Y. 10010

Diplomatic and Consular Officer Retired
1718 H St., N.W.
Washington, D.C. 20006
For retired members of the Foreign Service and other federal government agencies who have served overseas.

Federation Employment and Guidance Service
215 Park Ave. South
New York, N.Y. 10003
For handicapped, hard-to-place, or older workers.

Information and Counseling Service for Adults
Calvert and 23rd Sts.
Baltimore, Md. 21218

Jewish Vocational Service and Employment Centers
Branches in Chicago, Boston, Minneapolis, St. Paul, Kansas

City (Mo.), St. Louis, Newark, Buffalo, New York City, Cleveland, Cincinnati, Philadelphia, Houston. (See telephone directories for local addresses.)

National Conference of Forty-Plus Clubs of the U.S.
810 18th St., N.W.
Washington, D.C. 20006
For executives or professional men over forty years of age; handled by local clubs. Listing of local clubs free of charge.

Retired Officers Association
1616 I St., N.W.
Washington, D.C. 20006
For retired military officers.

Retired Patrolmen's Association of New York City
6 Maiden Lane
New York, N.Y. 10038

Retired Professor Registry
1785 Massachusetts Ave., N.W.
Washington, D.C. 20006
For academic and administrative personnel for colleges and universities, armed forces personnel, government officials, and some industrial personnel.

Vocational Advisory Service
432 Fourth Ave.
New York, N.Y. 10016

Vocational Guidance and Rehabilitation Service
1001 Huron Rd.
Cleveland, Ohio 44124

Woman's Educational and Industrial Union
264 Boylston St.
Boston, Mass. 02216
For seamstresses, practical nurses, waitresses, cooks, and general housekeepers; women over sixty are given place-

ment as companion-housekeepers for older people.

APPENDIX C
Health Associations

American Cancer Association
219 E. 42nd St.
New York, N.Y. 10017

American Heart Association
44 E. 23rd St.
New York, N.Y. 10010

American Foundation for the Blind
15 W. 16th St.
New York, N.Y. 10010
Provides information about resources for the blind and blind-deaf and also produces Talking Books.

American Diabetes Association
18 E. 48th St.
New York, N.Y. 10017

Arthritis Foundation 1212 Ave. of the Americas
New York, N.Y. 10036

Cancer Care, Inc., an affiliate of the National Cancer Foundation
1 Park Ave.
New York, N.Y. 10016
Provides counseling and financial aid in cases of advanced cancer.

National Easter Seal Society for Crippled Children and Adults
2023 West Ogden Ave.
Chicago, Ill. 60612
Provides services for the elderly with physical handicaps through its rehabilitation and treatment centers, and ther-

apy and visitor programs for the home-bound.

National Parkinson Foundation
135 E. 44th St.
New York, N.Y. 10017

Sex Information and Education Council of the United States (SIECUS)
1855 Broadway
New York, N.Y. 10023
Seeks to provide sexual material and information for professionals in the medical, social, and other related fields.

APPENDIX D
General Organizations Pertaining to Senior Citizens

American Aging Association
University of Nebraska Medical Center
Omaha, Neb.
Scientific group dedicated to promoting research in aging.

American Association of Homes for the Aging
529 14th St., N.W.
Washington, D.C. 20004
Represents nonprofit homes for the aging.

American Association of Retired Persons
1909 K St., N.W.
Washington, D.C. 20006
Perhaps the largest and most influential retirement organization. Membership open to

persons age fifty-five and above.

American Civil Liberties Union
22 E. 40th St.
New York, N.Y. 10016

The American Geriatrics Society
10 Columbus Circle
New York, N.Y. 10019
Made up of physicians.

American Nurses Association, Inc.
10 Columbus Circle
New York N.Y. 10019

American Nursing Home Association
(American Health Care Association)
1025 Connecticut Ave., N.W.
Washington, D.C. 20036
Represents commercial nursing home industry.

American Occupational Therapy Association
251 Park Ave. South
New York, N.Y. 10010

American Physical Therapy Association
1740 Broadway
New York, N.Y. 10019

American Psychological Association, Division of Adult Development and Aging
1200 17th St., N.W.
Washington, D.C. 20036

The Forum for Professionals and Executives
c/o The Washington School of Psychiatry
1610 New Hampshire Ave., N.W.
Washington, D.C. 20009

Gerontology Center
University of Southern California
Los Angeles, Calif. 90007

The Gerontological Society
1 Dupont Circle
Washington, D.C. 20036

Gray Panthers
6342 Greene St.
Philadelphia, Pa. 19144
Activist retirement group.

The Institute for Retired Professionals
The New School of Social Research
60 West 12th St.
New York, N.Y. 10011
Pioneers in providing activities for retired professional people.

The Institute of Lifelong Learning
Educational services of the American Association of Retired Persons.
Contact the Washington, D.C. AARP office for one located near you.

The International Federation on Aging
1909 K St., N.W.
Washington, D.C. 20006
Made up of organizations for the aged of several nations.

International Senior Citizens Association, Inc.
11753 Wilshire Blvd.
Los Angeles, Calif. 90025

National Association of Retired Federal Employees
1909 Q St., N.W.
Washington, D.C. 20009

National Association of Social Workers
2 Park Ave.
New York, N.Y. 10016

The National Association of State Units on Aging
Write local state office on aging for current address.
Lobbies for state agencies at the federal level.

The National Caucus on the Black Aged
1725 DeSales St., N.W.
Washington, D.C. 20036

National Council for Homemaker Services
1790 Broadway
New York, N.Y. 10019

National Council of Health Care Services
407 N St., S.W.
Washington, D.C. 20024
Representative for commercial nursing-home chains.

National Council of Senior Citizens
1911 K. St., N.W., Rm 202
Washington, D.C. 20005

National Council on the Aging
1828 L St., N.W., Suite 504
Washington, D.C. 20036

National Retired Teachers Association
1909 K. St., N.W.
Washington, D.C. 20006

National Tenants Organization
425 13th St., N.W., Suite 548
Washington, D.C. 20004
Offers representation to old people in public housing.

Older Women's Liberation (OWL)
National Chairperson of the Task Force on Older Women
National Organization for Women
1957 E. 73rd St.
Chicago, Ill. 60649
OWL is an offshoot of the National Organization for Women geared to special needs of women forty and older.

The Oliver Wendell Holmes Association
381 Park Ave. South
New York, N.Y. 10016
Promotes the intellectual concerns of senior citizens.

Retired Professional Action Group
200 P St., N.W., Suite 711
Washington, D.C. 20001
An investigative body.

Senior Advocates International
1825 K St., N.W.
Washington, D.C. 20006
Urban Elderly Coalition
c/o Office of Aging of New
York City
250 Broadway
New York, N.Y. 10017
Group formed to help obtain
funds for urban retired poor.

APPENDIX E
National, Regional, and State Offices on Aging

National

U.S. Administration on Aging
330 C St., S.W.
HEW South
Washington, D.C. 20201

Regional Offices

Region I (Conn., Maine, Mass., N.H., R.I., Vt.)
J.F. Kennedy Federal Bldg.
Government Center
Boston, Mass. 02203
Region II (N.J., N.Y., Puerto Rico, Virgin Islands)
26 Federal Plaza, SRS, AoA
New York, N.Y. 10007
Region III (Del., D.C., Md., Pa., Va., W. Va.)
P.O. Box 12900
Philadelphia, Pa. 12900

Region IV (Ala., Fla., Ga., Ky., Miss., N.C., S.C., Tenn.)
50 Seventh St., N.E., Rm. 404
Atlanta, Ga. 30323
Region V (Ill., Ind., Mich., Minn., Ohio, Wis.)
433 W. Van Buren, Rm. 712
New Post Office Bldg.
Chicago, Ill. 60607
Region VI (Ark., La., N. Mex., Okla., Tex.)
1114 Commerce St.
Dallas, Tex. 75202
Region VII (Iowa, Kans., Mo., Nebr.)
601 E. 12th St.
Kansas City, Mo. 64106
Region VIII (Colo., Mont., N. Dak., S. Dak., Utah, Wyo.)
19th and Stout Sts., Rm. 9017
Federal Office Bldg.
Denver, Colo. 80202
Region IX (Ariz., Calif., Hawaii, Nev., Samoa, Guam, T.T.)
50 Fulton St., Rm. 406
Federal Office Bldg.
San Francisco, Calif. 94102
Region X (Alaska, Idaho, Oreg., Wash.)
1319 2nd Ave., Mezzanine Floor
Arcade Bldg.
Seattle, Wash. 98101

State Offices on Aging

Includes Guam, Puerto Rico, Samoa, Trust Territory of the Pacific, and Virgin Islands.

Alabama
Commission on Aging
740 Madison Ave.
Montgomery 36104

Alaska
Office on Aging
Department of Health and Social Services
Pouch H
Juneau 99801

Arizona
Bureau on Aging
Department of Economic Security
2721 N. Central, Suite 800
South Tower
Phoenix 85004

Arkansas
Office on Aging
Department of Social and Rehabilitation Services
4313 W. Markham
Hendrix Hall
P.O. Box 2179
Little Rock 72203

California
Department of Aging
Health and Welfare Agency
918 J St.
Sacramento 95814

Colorado
Division of Services for the Aging
Department of Social Services
1575 Sherman St.
Denver 80203

Connecticut
Department of Aging
90 Washington St., Rm 312
Hartford 06115

Delaware
Division of Aging
Department of Health and Social Services
2407 Lancaster Ave.
Wilmington 19805

District of Columbia
Division of Services to the Aged
Department of Human Resources

1329 E Street, N.W.
Munsey Bldg., 10th Floor
Washington, D.C. 20004

Florida
Division on Aging
Department of Health and Rehabilitative Services
1323 Winewood Blvd.
Tallahassee 32301

Georgia
Office of Aging
Department of Human Resources
618 Ponce de Leon, Suite 301
Atlanta 30308

Guam
Office of Aging
Social Service Administration
Government of Guam
P.O. Box 2816
Agana 96910

Hawaii
Commission on Aging
1149 Bethel St., Rm 311
Honolulu 96813

Idaho
Office on Aging
Department of Special Services
Capital Annex #7
509 N. Fifth St.
Boise 83720

Illinois
Department on Aging
2401 W. Jefferson
Springfield 62762

Indiana
Commission on Aging and Aged
Graphic Arts Building
215 N. Senate Ave.
Indianapolis 46202

Iowa
Commission on the Aging
415 W. Tenth St.
Jewett Bldg.
Des Moines 50319

Kansas
Division of Social Services
Services for the Aging Section
Department of Social and Rehabilitation Services
State Office Bldg.
Topeka 66612

Kentucky
Aging Program Unit
Department for Human Resources
403 Wapping St.
Frankfort 40601

Louisiana
Bureau of Aging Services
Division of Human Resources
Health and Social and Rehabilitation Services Administration
P.O. Box 44282, Capital Station
Baton Rouge 70804

Maine
Services for Aging
Community Services Unit
Department of Health and Welfare
State House
Augusta 04330

Maryland
Commission on Aging
State Office Bldg.
1123 N. Eutaw St.
Baltimore 21201

Massachusetts
Executive Office of Elder Affairs
State Office Bldg.
18 Tremont St.
Boston 02109

Michigan
Office of Services to the Aging
1026 E. Michigan
Lansing 48912

Minnesota
Governor's Citizens Council on Aging

690 N. Robert St.
St. Paul 55101

Mississippi
Council on Aging
P.O. Box 5136, Fondren Station
Jackson 39216

Missouri
Office of Aging
Department of Community Affairs
505 Missouri Blvd.
Jefferson City 65101

Montana
Aging Services Bureau
Department of Social and Rehabilitation Services
P.O. Box 1723
Helena 59601

Nebraska
Commission on Aging
State House Station 94784
300 S. 17th St.
Lincoln 68509

Nevada
Division of Aging
Department of Human Resources
201 S. Fall Street, Rm 300, Nye Bldg.
Carson City 89701

New Hampshire
Council on Aging
P.O. Box 786
14 Depot St.
Concord 03301

New Jersey
Office on Aging
Department of Community Affairs
P.O. Box 2768
363 W. State St.
Trenton 08625

New Mexico
Commission on Aging
408 Galisteo—Villagra Building
Santa Fe 87501

New York
Office for the Aging
New York State Executive
Department
855 Central Ave.
Albany 12206
North Carolina
Governor's Coordinating
Council on Aging
Department of Human Re-
sources
Administration Bldg.
213 Hillsborough St.
Raleigh 27603
North Dakota
Aging Services
Social Services Board
Department of Social Services
State Capitol Bldg.
Bismarck 58501
Ohio
Commission on Aging
34 N. High St., Third Floor
Columbus 43215
Oklahoma
Special Unit on Aging
Department of Institutions
Social and Rehabilitative Ser-
vices
P.O. Box 25352, Capitol Sta-
tion
Oklahoma City 73125
Oregon
Program on Aging
Human Resources Depart-
ment
315 Public Service Bldg.
Salem 97310
Pennsylvania
Office for the Aging
Department of Public Welfare
Capitol Associates Bldg.
Seventh and Forster Sts.
Harrisburg 17120
Puerto Rico
Gericulture Commission
Department of Social Services

Apartado 11697
Santurce 00910
Rhode Island
Division on Aging
Department of Community
Affairs
150 Washington St.
Providence 02903
Samoa
Government of American
Samoa
Office of the Governor
Pago Pago, American Samoa
96920
South Carolina
Commission on Aging
915 Main St.
Columbia 29201
South Dakota
Program on Aging
Department of Social Services
St. Charles Hotel
Pierre 57501
Tennessee
Commission on Aging
510 Gay St.
Capital Towers, Floor B-3,
Suite B-1
Nashville 37319
Texas
Governor's Committee on Ag-
ing
P.O. Box 12786,
Capitol Station
Austin 78711
Trust Territory of the Pacific
Office of Aging
Community Development
Division
Government of the Trust
Territory of the Pacific Is-
lands
Saipan, Mariana Islands
96950
Utah
Division of Aging
Department of Social Services

345 S. 6th East
Salt Lake City 84102

Vermont
Office on Aging
Department of Human Services
126 Main St.
Montpelier 05602

Virgin Islands
Commission on Aging
P.O. Box 539
Charlotte Amalie
St. Thomas 00801

Virginia
Office on Aging
Division of State Planning and Community Affairs
9 N. 12th St.
Richmond 23219

Washington
Office on Aging
Department of Social and

Health Services
P.O. Box 1788—M.S. 45-2
410 W. Fifth
Olympia 98504

West Virginia
Commission on Aging
State Capitol
Charleston 25305

Wisconsin
Division on Aging
Department of Health and Social Services
1 W. Wilson St., Rm 686
Madison 53702

Wyoming
Aging Services
Department of Health and Social Services
Division of Public Assistance and Social Services
State Office Bldg.
Cheyenne 82002

INDEX

activism. *See* senior advocacy
advocacy. *See* senior advocacy
aging, 97–100
Aging Is Not for Sissies,
    11–12
American Association of Re-
    tired Persons (AARP),
    92, 108, 109
*Annual Register of Grant Sup-
    port*, 144
annuities, as investments, 69
appliance repair, as second career,
    86–87
auto mechanics, as second career,
    88

bankruptcy, effect on pension
    funds, 38–39
Best's Insurance Reports, 109
Blue Cross, 108, 109
Blue Shield, 108, 109
bonds, as investment, 68
bookkeeping, as second career,
    87
budget, retirement, 23–32
Bureau of Labor Statistics, 26
bus transportation, 150–52
business consultant, as second
    career, 85–86
Butler, Robert, 15, 16, 99,
    106–7

*Catalog of Federal Domestic
    Assistance, The*, 143
Central States Teamsters Pension
    Fund, 39
changing jobs, effect on pension,
    41, 61
clothing costs, 26, 27, 31
Commerce Clearing House, 39

Consumer Price Index, 28
Consumer Reports, 104
contributions, budgeting for, 26,
    27, 30–31
Cottin, Lou, 12–14

day care for children, as second
    career, 89
death of spouse, 72–73, 100–101,
    see also widowhood
Department of Defense Referral
    Program, 92
depression, psychological,
    99–100
diet. *See* nutrition

early retirement, 34
education, for second career,
    83–85
Employee Retirement Income
    Security Act, 39
employment agencies, 91
employment counseling, 167–68
employment programs, 165–66
*Estimating Your Social Security
    Check*, 55
EXPO, 12–14

food, budgeting for, 26, 27, 28–
    29, *see also* nutrition
Food and Drug Administration,
    97
Forty-Plus Club, 92
Foster Grandparents Program, 153
Foundation of Grants Index, 144
*Funk & Wagnalls Guide to Per-
    sonal Money Management*
    (Colburn), 68

gerontological medicine, 158
gifts, budgeting for, 26, 27, 30–
    31
government funding, 142–44
Gray Panthers, 102, 117, 123
Great Depression, 156
Guardian Life Insurance Com-
    pany, 108

health, 15–16, 94–113, 158
health associations, 169
health insurance, 94–113
    Medicaid, 107–8
    Medicare, 103–7
    national, 157–8
    private, 108–13
holographic wills, 74
home ownership, 70
Homemaking Service, 152
hot meals dining sites, 145–46
housing costs, 26, 27, 30

income tax. *See* taxes
indemnity benefits, 111
Individual Retirement Account
    (IRA), 57, 61–66
inflation, 45–52, 64, 69
insurance
    budgeting for, 26, 27, 31
    health, 103–13, 157–58
    life, 70
    mail-order, 110
    for pension funds, 57, 58–59
insurance agent, choice of, 110
Internal Revenue Service (IRS)
    67, 71
investment, 45–52
IRA (Individual Retirement
    Account), 57, 61–66
IRS (Internal Revenue Service),
    67, 71

Javits, Jacob, 38

Keogh Plan, 57, 61–65, 66–67
Kuhn, Maggie, 102, 123

letters to the editor, senior advo-
    cacy and, 130
"life change index," 99–100
life insurance, 70
loneliness, 99

mandatory retirement, 155–57
Mature Temps, Inc., 92
Mead, Margaret, 92–93

Meals on Wheels program, 147
Medicaid, 107–8
medical costs, 26, 27, 30
Medically Needed Only (MNO)
    funding, 107–8
Medicare, 103–7
middle class, retirement threat
    to, 16–19

Nader, Ralph, 38, 157
National Council of Senior Citi-
    zens (NCSC), 108
national health insurance, 157–58
National Institute on Aging, 99
National Organization for Women
    (NOW), 19
National Retired Teachers Associ-
    ation (NRTA), 92
news media, senior advocacy and,
    127–31
newsletters, 140–41
Not Quite Ready to Retire
    (David), 85
nursing homes, 158
nutrition, 15–16, 97
Nutritionmobile, 146–47

Older Americans Act, 144, 145,
    149

Pension Benefit Guaranty Corpo-
    ration, 58
pensions, 37–42, 56–61, 157
    company, 57–59
    how to investigate, 59–60
personal-care costs, 26, 27, 30
political involvement. *See* senior
    advocacy
poverty, 4–6, 7–8, 11, 14–16
press. *See* news media
promotion, effects on pension,
    41

radio stations, senior advocacy
    and, 130–31
real estate
    as investment, 68–69

as second career, 88
recreation costs, 26, 27
rent control, 159
Retired Senior Volunteer Programs, 153
retirement, early, 34
Retirement Handbook, The, 11
retirement income credits, 71
retirement, mandatory, 155–57

sales, as second career, 88
savings, 23
    budgeting for, 26, 27
savings accounts, 24, 43–44, 69
second career. *See* working after retirement
self-employment. *see also* working after retirement
    pensions and, 57
    Social Security and, 53, 54, 80
senior advocacy, 114–33
    courses in, 139–40
    strategy, 121–27
    theory behind, 153–54
    in Ventura County, 134–35
senior clubs, 122
Senior Corps of Retired Executives (SCORE), 86
Senior discounts, 152
senior foundations, 159
"senior survival services" program, 147–49
service benefits, 111
Shore, Warren, 35, 36–37
Sixth Annual Conference on Employee Benefits (1972), 38
Skill Bank, 141–42
Small Business Administration (SBA), 86
Social Security, 2, 3, 33–37, 52–55, 156, 157, 159
    eligibility, 53–54
    second career and, 79–81
Social Security: The Fraud in Your Future (Shore), 35

Sommers, Tish, 19
SSI (Supplemental Security Income), 55–56, 107
State Employment Services Office, 91
stocks, as investment, 68
suicide, 20–22
Supplemental Security Income (SSI) 55–56, 107
Survival Gardens, 153
Survivalmobile fleet, 149–50
survivor's benefits, 42–43

Tax Facts, 71
"Tax Information on Individual Retirement Savings Programs," 67
tax preparation, as second career, 87
taxes, 71
    budgeting for, 26, 27
    estate, 75
    on IRA, 66
    property, 159
    self-employment, 54
    Social Security, 52–53, 54
Tel Med Tapes, 153
television stations, senior advocacy and, 131
training, for second career, 83–85
transportation, 149–52, 158–59
    budgeting for, 26, 27
    public, 120, 150–52
tutoring, as second career, 89

unions, 38, 39, 59
United Mine Workers Welfare and Retirement Fund, 39
U.S. Department of Commerce, 28
U.S. Department of Labor, 58, 156
U.S. Public Health Service, 20
U.S. Senate Special Committee on Aging, 15
utility rate reductions, 152, 159

Ventura county, senior programs and, 7, 121, 127, 134–54
vesting, 40–41, 57–58
volunteer programs, 165–66

What's Wrong with Your Life Insurance (Dacey), 70
Why Survive? Being Old in America (Butler), 15
widowhood, 19–22. *See also* death of spouse

wills, 73–75
working after retirement, 76, 77–93

"Your Federal Income Tax," 71
Your Insurance Handbook (Guarino & Trubo), 70
Your Social Security Rights and Responsibilities, 55